COMPLETING THE
VANDAL FAMILY PICTURE

COMPLETING THE
VANDAL FAMILY PICTURE

An Account of the History of the Vandal Family from 1530 to 2012

Including information from and the memories of
Carl George Vandal, Australia
Patricia J Smith, USA and
Mary Susan Findlay, USA but formerly of Canada

R O B   V A N D A L

authorHOUSE®

AuthorHouse™ UK Ltd.
1663 Liberty Drive
Bloomington, IN 47403 USA
www.authorhouse.co.uk
Phone: 0800.197.4150

Published by AuthorHouse   07/25/2014

ISBN: 978-1-4969-8508-8 (sc)
ISBN: 978-1-4969-8509-5 (e)

Library of Congress Control Number: 2014911948

CONTENTS

ACKNOWLEDGEMENTS

I would like to thank Carl George Vandal, Australia, for his information about and his memories of family members that he had known.

I owe a debt of gratitude to Bjarne A. Kofoed (of DK-8732 Hovedgård) who, from his database of 6000 Bornholm ancestors, sent me a 159 page document with all the ancestors he could find for our grandfather Jørgen Michael Larsen Wandahl.

I thank the scotlandspeople.gov.uk website for being able access with ease, Parish records, Census Returns, Valuation Rolls and Statutory Records of Births, Marriages and Deaths.

Intimations in the Greenock Telegraph
Death of Benjamin Jemmott, 21.4.1892
Death of VANDAL Joan Fisher, 23.8.1901
Birth of VANDAL Margaret Anders 11.1.1906
Death of VANDAL Margaret Anders 7.9.1906

The several images of street scenes of Old Greenock have been used by kind permission of the McLean Museum and Art Gallery, Inverclyde Council, Greenock.

I thank Mr. Zac Harrison for permission to use the photograph of Vic32 (believed to be the sole-surviving, working Clyde Puffer).

The images "Preparing to sail" and "The Glencloy discharging a cargo" have been used by kind permission of the Ballast Trust, Johnstone, Scotland.

THE VANDAL FAMILY IN SCOTLAND

INTRODUCTION

It is very rare in a working-class family that anyone keeps written records (or even a personal diary) of the family history though there are usually retold family stories of family members, occasions or incidents which might or might not be retold correctly. In our family, the Vandal family, from the late 1800's and early 1900's, several unusual family stories have circulated but there has also been some mystery concerning our family at that time since certain family members, occasions or incidents were regarded as 'less than reputable' and therefore not 'spoken about' and now that the older members of the family have passed away there is no longer a chance of substantiating existing family stories. Therefore, starting from a known fact or date, what is now left to us is to dig into existing parish records and the more substantial statutory records to hopefully work out reasonably correct assumptions from the information they contain. Family history, therefore, could be just a collection of dry dates but if these dates can be tied in, even tenuously, with historical and social changes then family history becomes much more interesting.

In Scotland, before 1855, registers recording births, baptisms, the reading of banns before marriage, marriages, deaths and burials of those of the Protestant faith were kept by individual parishes of the Established Church (Church of Scotland) and those of the Roman Catholic faith by individual parishes of the Roman Catholic Church. Parish record keeping commenced in different years in different parishes and unfortunately over the years many of the records were damaged by poor storage or were lost or destroyed. The parish minister or the session clerk usually maintained these registers, but no standard format was employed, and record keeping varied enormously from parish to parish.[1]

There was also a charge for registration in Church of Scotland registers therefore many people with restricted incomes did not bother to have 'less important' events recorded.

Parish Records of marriages tend only to give the date and the name of the persons being married and do not include the parents of the bride or groom. With such sparse information and with so many people having similar names it can be difficult to decide on the correct connection of one person to another person.

For example Grandpa (Robert) Stevenson's father was a George Stevenson whose father was a Robert Stevenson and since there are in the Parish Records numerous people with the name Robert Stevenson and George Stevenson and no other unique distinguishing characteristic, it makes it impossible with certainty to find the correct one.

The major changes to record keeping in the middle 1800's were the collection of population Census Returns and the keeping of Statutory Records of Births, Marriages and Deaths to replace the previous and sometimes rudimentary Parish Records.

A Statutory Record of Birth records place of birth and the name and occupation of both parents. A Statutory Record of Marriage includes not only the names of those being married but also their employment and the names of both sets of parents, alive or deceased. A Statutory Record of Death contains the name, age and place of death of deceased as well as name and occupation of parents and name and residence of informant. The Census records all the residents, and their ages and occupations, at a particular address at the time of census taking. All this information helps in the correct identification of relationships. I have, as far as possible, accessed Statutory Records to make the family history and tree as accurate

1

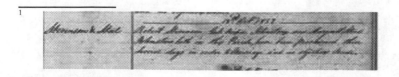

as I can though in order to trace our tree back as far as possible I have also accessed what parish records I have been able to find.

There was also the introduction of Compulsory Education. In the early 1800's, before compulsory education, very few working class people could read or write. They would verbally give their names and other relevant information to the registrar or other official who would write it down as he thought it should be written and the informant would be unable to correct. Therefore, even in official records, there may be a variety of spellings of names.

Much of the early history of the Vandal family in Scotland, takes place in Greenock in the latter half of the 1800's and it has been shaped by the events and the social changes of those times and that town.

In the late 18th century and early 19th century the ship builders, owners and merchants of Greenock founded, with their increasing prosperity, a new and more admirable town but they did it side by side with the dingy, crooked, irregular and congested layout of the old narrow, unclean streets, aimless lanes and huddled hovels of the east and middle town. Many town streets were only partly paved or totally unpaved and ashes and filth of every description including sewage was regularly thrown into the middle (the midden[2]) of the streets where it could seep through the ground surface into the wells from which the public water supply was drawn. By the 1850's, although Greenock was an important manufacturing town and port, visitors to the Clyde coast resorts had to walk from the newly opened

---

[2]   From the 11th till the 17th century, many refugees to England, Wales and Scotland were from the Low Countries; particularly Flemish skilled weavers and textile workers who fled Dutch-speaking Flanders as a result of floods, overpopulation and warfare.

In the late Middle Ages, the Hanseatic League had a trade network along the coast of Northern Europe to Scotland and merchants often used an amalgam of Scots and Dutch as a common language. Many words, in the Scots' dictionary have come from the use of this "lingua franca". For example the word "midden", (meaning "trash can/dustbin/rubbish tip") comes from the time when many town and city streets had open sewers running through them into which all kinds of waste was thrown: butchers would also throw their offal into the street in front of their shops. The words "Throw the rubbish into the middle of the street" in Dutch is "Gooi het afval (offal) in de midden (middle) van de straat (street)".

railway station[3] to the steamboat pier through an unpleasant lane in one of the most squalid areas in the heart of Old Greenock.

By the middle of the 19th century, displaced from the Highlands and from Ireland, there was a rapid influx of migrants looking for work in the new factories and heavy industries of Greenock, Paisley, Glasgow, Coatbridge and Dundee. This population explosion created such a demand for accommodation that the provision of proper housing in these growing urban centres was almost an impossibility and this caused ill health and disease in the already overcrowded, one-roomed houses that had to share a common water closet and a common sink. It is on record that in 1867 one village in Fife had only two water closets for a population of 2,000.

Living conditions throughout the country in general for working people were so bad that 27 housing acts were passed in the second half of the 19th century. Probably the most significant act, however, was "The Artisans' and Labourers' Dwellings Improvement Act 1875". In 1877, Greenock Corporation was among the first of the town corporations to take advantage of this Act: in the lower parts of the town 605 dilapidated houses, reported to be unfit for human habitation, were acquired and demolished and 2,700 persons were displaced. Under these Improvement Schemes ancient dilapidated streets, lanes and buildings in the town centre disappeared, and by the end of the 1800's most of the old mediaeval town of Greenock had vanished in an effort to improve the living conditions and the health of the population.

---

[3]   In the early 19th century the railway system was still being built and the main mode of transport was on foot or by horse and cart along very poorly made and maintained roads, or by river in wooden barges and ships. Work was more important than leisure and the length of the working day was 14 to 16 hours. Daily life was monotonous and routine for the poor and, until the growth of professional football in the late 19th century and the music hall and the cinema in the early 20th century, they had few forms of popular entertainment outside the culture of heavy drinking in dens and taverns.

Our Family's Irish Ancestors in Scotland

GRANNY VANDAL

Granny Vandal's parents appear to have settled in Paisley during the early to middle 1800's and she was born Isabella McConnachie in 1867 in Paisley. Her father, Andrew McConnachie (boatman) and her mother, Isabella Cashore married in 1863 in St. Mirrin's Church Paisley. (Neither was able to read nor write but made their mark on their marriage certificate.) The address in the marriage record is 9 Mid Lane Paisley. This marriage certificate also records the paternal parents (Granny Vandal's grandparents) as Andrew McConnachie (labourer) and his wife Mary Connor (deceased) and the maternal parents as Thomas Cashore (or Cichore), a shoemaker[4] whose wife was Jane Oliver (deceased).

---

[4]   Until the middle 1800s, nearly every village had, at least, one skilled shoemaker who made hand-stitched shoes for individual customers. During the Napoleonic wars of the early 1800s, because the British Army of 250,000 men required a large supply of boots, machinery was adapted to make boots and shoes in newly built factories.

Unskilled, casual labourers (even children) were trained to produce these machine made boots and shoes faster and cheaper than individual craftsmen and many time-served, craftsmen shoemakers became unemployed.

The 1871 census records that her paternal and maternal grandparents, and her parents Andrew and Isabella McConnachie, were born in Ireland[5]. The family address in the record is now 58 Back Sneddon, close to Paisley Harbour.

There were, I believe, possibly four children from the marriage; Andrew, born 1865, Isabella (Granny Vandal) born 1867, William, born 1869 and a child born in 1872. (However, the 1871 census records a John McConnachie aged 13 as a son but this would have meant that he was 5 years old at the time of his parents' wedding.).

The records appear to show that Isabella McConnachie's (Granny Vandal's) early life was certainly not easy, though to the best of my memory this was never mentioned in the family.

Her elder brother Andrew, born 1865, died in 1867, aged 2 years 8 months; her younger brother William, born 1869, died in1870 just 11 months old and evidence strongly suggests that another child died at birth since, in April 1872 when Granny Vandal was just 5 years old, her mother died of childbed fever. Almost exactly a year later, in 1873, her father died.

These events left Isabella (Granny Vandal) as an orphan since she was the only member of that immediate family to have survived.

From the census record of 1881 it would appear that she was raised by James Fleming and his wife Catherine who had been born in Ireland. Because the information is only Ireland with no other place name I have been unable to locate birth or marriage records for the Flemings. The death certificate of 1903 for James Fleming records his parents as being a James Fleming (spirit dealer, deceased) and a Helen Bonnar. The maiden surname of James Fleming's wife Catherine was McConnachie. She is recorded in

---

[5]   Catholic Irish families suffered from the prejudices of a non-church-going, presbyterian population who perhaps did not regularly attend church, but required the presence of a minister as essential for performing the ceremonies of marriage, christening, baptism and burial. Catholic Irish families were often portrayed as uncivilized, drunken, lazy characters and prejudice and discrimination combined to keep the Catholic Irish at the bottom of the heap. Even recruitment to certain occupations in the West of Scotland depended on a religious basis.

several records as being an 'aunt' but it is not entirely clear from the records whether Catherine was or was not the sister of Granny Vandal's father.

Isabella's Uncle Owen, who had reported her father's death, died in 1884. In that same year, when Granny Vandal was 17 years old, her maternal grandfather, Thomas Cashore, died aged 70 in Paisley Burgh Poorhouse.

In 1884, when she was approximately 16 or 17 years of age, Isabella (Granny Vandal) married for the first time. In 1889 her first child, Andrew, died of diphtheria at the age of 1 year and 10 months. In 1893, by the age of 26, she was recorded as being a widow. Her Aunt Catherine with whom, according to the 1881 census, she had lodged and who had reported the birth of the three children, died in 1898.

The family story is that when Granny Vandal's second marriage was to a non Catholic, her father's relatives refused to acknowledge her. That could be true but records show that many of her close family, the McConnachies, were dead by that time.

However the following evidence, collated from an application to be admitted to the Burgh Poorhouse, Paisley, made in 1881 by Thomas Cashore, Granny Vandal's maternal grandfather, appears to show that though there may have been some truth in the story of her being shunned by relatives it was the Cashore family who refused to acknowledge her and not the McConnachies.

Thomas Cashore, my maternal great-great grandfather, was born circa 1813 in Wexford[6], Co. Wexford, Ireland to William[7] Cashore, a soldier, and his wife Isabella McMillan.

Thomas was a shoemaker to trade. He was married to Jane Oliver. They had five children, all born in Co. Donegal, Ireland, therefore Thomas and his wife must have moved there before the birth of their children. His eldest daughter Isabella, my great grandmother, was born in 1837; his

---

[6]   The Rebellion of 1798 was confined mainly to the counties of Antrim, Down, and Wexford. It has been regarded as amongst the bloodiest conflicts in recent Irish history though none of the regional rebellions that broke out was as destructive of life and property as that which occurred in County Wexford. The fighting was a frightened response by the rebels to the authorities' search for arms and conspirators and in Wexford it produced several tragic massacres of those assumed to be loyal to the government side, almost all of them Anglicans. These massacres have been regarded as proof that the conflict in Wexford was sectarian
The fact that much of the violence that followed the rebellion was blatantly sectarian drove a much deeper wedge between the Anglican and Catholic communities of that county than the rebellion itself had done. Sectarian tensions became endemic in Wexford and sectarian violence was still part of life there as late as the 1840s. Anglicans and Catholics emigrated in large numbers, from about the 1820's, to the industrial cities of Glasgow, Liverpool, Manchester and London and onwards to the United States and Canada. This may have eased tensions somewhat but it would not be a pleasant time to grow up or live in Wexford in the early 1800's, or to be a British soldier stationed there or to be a member of a soldier's family.

[7]   Unfortunately essential regimental records relating to the Irish yeomanry and militia were destroyed in the Four Courts fire during the Irish Civil War of 1921-1922. This makes it difficult to research information on William Cashore and his regiment but it would be highly unlikely in the 1790's that an Irish person of the Roman Catholic faith would be a soldier in the British Army and have the first name, William

eldest son, William was born in 1840, Elizabeth in 1843, Sarah in 1845, James in 1846 and Jane who was born in 1848.

His wife, Jane died in 1850. After her death I believe they, just like thousands of others, left Ireland because of the famine, the starvation, famine-related diseases, and scenes of unimaginable mass suffering they had witnessed and endured.

In 1881, after several years of living as an itinerant lodger in Paisley, Thomas had to list his children on his application to be admitted into the Burgh Poorhouse, Paisley[8]. He omitted one name from the list, his eldest daughter Isabella Cashore, born circa 1837, who nine years previously in April 1872, had died of childbed fever.

In 1863, Isabella had married Andrew McConnachie in St. Mirrin's Church, Paisley according to the forms of the Roman Catholic Church. Since the marriage certificate records the name of her father as Thomas Cashore and the name of her mother as Jane Cashore, née Oliver, she was most certainly his daughter.

The other Cashore family members did not marry in The Roman Catholic Church and the sons served in the British Army. This strongly suggests, but is not absolute proof, that the family were Protestant. Therefore it is just

---

[8]   The National Health Service in Britain was inaugurated in 1948. Before that time the rich could buy good medical help, but many others depended on charity. If people needed medical care they had to be able to pay the doctor or do without or claim poor relief from the parish or enter the parish poorhouse. In Scotland all applications for Poor Relief would be carefully examined by an Inspector of the Poor who was an employee of the parish. Poor relief was generally confined to the old, the infirm, the disabled or the mentally ill and could be given in the form of cash or in kind, or in a poorhouse set up to shelter the sick or destitute, but not the able-bodied for whom relief was rare. People ended-up in the poorhouse for a variety of reasons. Usually it was because they were too poor, too old or too ill to support themselves. This may have been caused by lack of work during periods of high unemployment, or having no family willing or able to provide care for them when they became elderly or chronically sick. Most poorhouses had a small infirmary room or block providing free medical treatment intended solely for the care of sick residents. The eventual admission of non-paupers to these infirmaries marked the beginnings of the national state-funded medical service for those who would not otherwise be able to afford it.

possible that it was Isabella McConnachie (née Cashore), Granny Vandal's mother who, because she had married a Roman Catholic, was disowned by her family, the Cashores, and that the confusion arose because Granny Vandal and her mother were both named Isabella McConnachie.

Although several of her brothers and sisters were married and lived in Paisley, none of them appears to have wanted to, or been able to take their sister's orphaned 5 year old daughter Isabella (Granny Vandal) into their care.

William served as a soldier and on leaving military service he married Sarah McLachlan in Paisley in 1878 according to the forms of the Free Church of Scotland. Elizabeth married William Parkhill in Paisley in 1866 according to the forms of the Church of Scotland.

Sarah married Thomas Eaglesom in Paisley in 1871 according to the forms of the Evangelical Union. Jane married William Scollan in Paisley in 1869 according to the forms of the Scottish Episcopalian Church. James was a soldier serving in India.[9] He retired to Paisley but remained unmarried.

In the census of 1881 the Fleming family are recorded as living in a dilapidated slum area of central Greenock. 2, Longwell Close, a narrow passage running parallel to

---

[9] I have been unable to find out any details of military service for James Cashore but I think that he probably served in one or other of the following regiments since these recruited in Scotland, were deployed in India or had Irish members. (a) In 1851, 358 of 696 members of the Royal Scots Fusiliers were Irish. (b) In 1857, the 93rd (Highland) Regiment of Foot embarked for service 12½ years in India before sailing for home. (c) In the 1860s the 91st (Argyllshire Highlanders) Regiment of Foot counted 501 Englishmen and 323 Irishmen in their ranks and only 241 Scots. (d) The 94th Regiment of Foot served in India between 1838 and 1854, again between 1857 and 1868 and yet again between 1899 and 1908. (e) The King's Own Scottish Borderers served in Ireland (1872-75), in India (1875-81) and Afghanistan (1878-80).

William Street, and connecting Cathcart Street with Shaw Street. The Close derived its name from a deep well that was believed to have been dug in the 17th century. In the surrounding streets few houses were connected to the sewer system and sewage, drainage and stagnant water lay everywhere. It was recorded by historians of that time that the Close was not much of a thoroughfare except for those living in the area and that these people were of the "poorest class".

This was one of the first areas in Greenock to be improved under "The Artisans' and Labourers' Dwellings Improvement Act 1875" that, among other things, set down minimum requirements of size, space and sanitation for the newly built housing. For instance, each new house had to have a lavatory (water closet) and a fresh water tap.

The tenements of the Close, with their dilapidated and insanitary living conditions, were condemned and demolished to make way to much improved and more sanitary buildings. The Close was converted into a "modern thoroughfare" and renamed Duff Street, in recognition of John Duff, a local Baillie (town councillor).

Since the 1881 census record shows that Isabella McConnachie (Granny Vandal) and her relatives lived in Longwell Close before it was demolished, rebuilt and renamed as Duff Street, it would seem unlikely that Granny Vandal's family would have had any "money" to leave her but records indicate that the family were able to move to the improved, rebuilt accommodation in the same area. The "money" that Granny Vandal was supposed (according to the family story) to have "inherited" may have come from her first husband.

I was aware that that Granny Vandal had been married previously but I was under the impression that her first married surname was McConnachie However her death record in 1942 produced two former surnames, McConnachie and Jemmott; it also gave her father's occupation as a steam lighterman though in the record of her marriage to Benjamin Jemmott, her father's occupation is recorded as labourer.

Using the surname Jemmott, I found a record of the marriage, in 1884 at St Lawrence Roman Catholic Church, Cartsdyke, Greenock, of Bella

McConnachie, spinster, to a Benjamin Jemmott, ship's steward. According to the marriage record Benjamin was 30 years old and Bella was 19. However 19 from 1884 is 1864/5 and this date does not tie in with the year of Bella's (Granny Vandal's) birth record, July 1867 nor with her recorded age of 13 in the census of 1881. Therefore it would appear that Bella was only 16 or 17 when she first married.

William Street

The marriage certificate records Bella's (Granny Vandal) parents as Andrew McConnachie, labourer and Isabella McConnachie, m.s. Cartshore (Cashore/Cashare) and Benjamin's parents as John Jemmott, joiner, and Adelaide Jemmott, m.s. Porter. At the time of the marriage it is recorded that the parents of both Bella and Benjamin were deceased and, unusual for a bride and groom, the same address is given for both, 1 William Street, Greenock.

Their first child, Andrew was born in 1887 at 1, William Street, Greenock. The birth record shows that his father, Benjamin Jemmott, was a ship's steward but the birth was reported by Catherine Fleming, the child's grand aunt who, according to the birth record, could not write but could only make her mark.

A daughter, Mary Adelaide, (Aunt Mary) was born in 1888 at 1, William Street, Greenock. Again the birth record shows that her father, Benjamin Jemmott, was a ship's steward and again the birth was reported by Catherine Fleming, her grand aunt.

The family appear to have moved house between 1888 and 1889 when, at the age of two, Andrew

Shaw Street (before improvement)

died of diphtheria. On this occasion Benjamin Francis Jemmott's signature is on the death record and the address is now 50 Shaw Street, Greenock.

Their second daughter, Elizabeth (Aunt Lizzie), was born in 1890 at 50 Shaw Street, Greenock and her birth certificate records her father, Benjamin Jemmott, as being a ship's steward. Again the birth was reported by Catherine Fleming, the baby's great aunt.

Shaw Street (after improvement)

In the late 18th century, at the corner of Shaw Street above the grocer's shop owned by Mr. Edward McCallum, there was a busy tavern in which many of the Council meetings were held. This is given as a suggestion that Council business was perhaps of lesser importance and that Town Councillors of former times were perhaps less "dignified" than those of today. The building in which the business of the council was conducted was still standing in the early 19th Century.

After the 1875 Act there were improvements to some buildings on the north side of Shaw Street and the south side of the street, running westwards from Cross-shore Street to William Street, was entirely re-built. Many of the displaced structures were at one time important both as business premises and as private residences.

The 1891 census appears to show that several households in Shaw Street had boarders and that at least one possibly had a servant. (A resident, having a different surname and therefore apparently not a family member, living with the household at 59 Shaw Street is recorded as being a general servant.)

The move to 50, Shaw Street and the length of residence there seems to show an improvement in the family finances possibly because of marriage to Benjamin Jemmott. This census also records Isabella Jemmott (married), with her children Mary and Elizabeth, lodging (apparently) at 50, Shaw Street, Greenock with James Fleming, as head of the household, and his wife, Catherine.

The assumption is that James Fleming was recorded as being the head of the household because at the time of the census he was the adult male person living there. It is possible that this, and the fact that succeeding generations of the family have been given the name James Fleming (Vandal), may have given rise to the idea that Granny Vandal was related in some way to the Fleming family of Greenock. (That family owned Fleming and Reid Woollen Mills, and wool shops).

This seems less than likely or at the very least a 'far-out' connection because James Fleming is recorded on some occasions as being a boatman or lighterman and on other occasions as being a general labourer. Several documents also record the words "James Fleming, his X mark" which indicates that he could neither read nor write and his death certificate records his father as being a James Fleming (spirit dealer, deceased).

From the various official documents it would appear that in the 25 years between 1884 and 1909 the family lived at 10 different addresses. This, and the fact that Grandpa Vandal is recorded in the 1905 Valuation Roll[10] as being a Tenant/Occupier, would suggest that the properties were rented and not owned by the family.

Most, if not all, of this would be private or local authority rented accommodation since very few working class or lower middle class people could afford, or even aspired, to buy a house. Rented accommodation, private as well as Council Housing, was the norm in

---

[10] Valuation Rolls record every kind of building, structure or property, from tenements to mansions and country estates, in Scotland and contain the name of the tenant and the occupier, of all social classes, who lived at each address and whether they owned or rented the property. In the Roll the named person is usually the head of the household but unlike the census records, the Rolls do not contain full lists of family members. Rolls also record the rent that was paid for the house or flat, and also the rateable value of the property.

Scotland right up until the 1980's when people were given the right to buy Council houses.

Benjamin Jemmott, Granny Vandal's first husband, was lost at sea. The census of 1891 does not record him as being present with the family and an intimation in The Greenock Telegraph dated 21.4.1892, records that Benjamin Jemmott, a cook from Greenock, was lost with the barque 'Cavour'[11] off the Galway coast on 9th February 1892 on the homeward journey from Pensacola, Florida to Greenock.

There are very few Scottish records of the name Jemmott; there are more in England. In the marriage record of 1884 the name of Benjamin Jemmott's father is recorded as John Jemmott (deceased) and his mother as Adelaide Porter (deceased).

In 1889, Benjamin reported the death of his son Andrew. I have not yet found any information of when he came to be in Scotland or how he met and married Bella McConnachie (Granny Vandal).

It is also information gleaned from the census records that could suggest possible reasons for the family story that Granny Vandal owned a boarding house or had property which she just gave away. In the 1871 census, when Granny Vandal was just 4 years old, her father Andrew is recorded as being head of the household but James Caloni, his son Robert and his daughter Catherine are also recorded as being boarders. In the 1881 census, Maria Brown, a Hawker, was recorded as a boarder in Longwell Close with the Fleming family.

In the census of 1891, Bella McConnachie (Granny Vandal) apparently lodged with her uncle, James Fleming and his wife however, in the census of 1901, James Fleming who was by that time a widower, lodged with Grandpa and Granny Vandal. It would seem that, either because of a

---

[11] When I was clearing my mother's house I found this ship in a bottle. I could not initially understand why it was there but it is possible that it is supposed to be the sailing ship 'Cavour', though this cannot now be confirmed, and that it was given to Granny Vandal by her first husband, Benjamin Jemmott. It is certainly the type of naïve art indulged in by early sailors to pass the time on a long voyage.

general lack of accommodation or because a family was attempting to earn some extra or essential cash, boarders were an accepted part of daily living.

In 1893, Bella Jemmott (Granny Vandal) is recorded as being widowed and still living in Shaw Street. After she married Carl Larsen Vandal (Grandpa Vandal) the family moved to 45, Rue End Street where, in 1894, their first son, George Larsen Vandal, was born. It is a reasonable assumption that after her marriage to Grandpa Vandal her aunt and uncle, Catherine and James Fleming, continued to live, at least for a short time, at Shaw Street.

Rue End Street

In the 1905 Valuation Rolls, George Vandal, Boatman, is recorded as being Tenant/Occupier (NOT owner) of a boarding house at 49, Rue End Street, Greenock. The family lived there between 1904 and 1906/7 before they moved to 15, Moss Street in Paisley.

In the 1911 census Isabella Vandal is recorded as working 'on her own account' as a common lodging house keeper at an eight room house in 3, New Sneddon Street, Paisley and these facts could possibly explain the family story that Granny Vandal had owned a boarding house that she left to the occupants.

The death record for Catherine Fleming, James' wife, is dated 1898 and gives her age as 54 (therefore, by calculation, a birth date of 1844) and gives her father's name as Andrew McConnachie, a labourer but her mother's maiden name as Mary McCabe whereas Connor is recorded as the maiden name of the mother of Granny Vandal's father.

This, I initially thought, was a possible mistake by James Fleming the informant since it would suggest that Catherine Fleming was not the sister of Granny Vandal's father. However, for whatever reason, it would appear that some information given for record-keeping was believed knowledge and not always accurate. Catherine's maiden surname, McConnachie, would appear to indicate that she was related in some way to Bella McConnachie (Granny Vandal). The information in the 1891 census record suggests that Catherine Fleming (McConnachie) was born circa 1844 in Ireland.

The McConnachie family were probably among those Irish emigrants who fled Ireland because of the potato famine[12] of 1846 to 1850.

---

[12]   In 1845, 1846, 1847 and 1848 the potato crop in Ireland was destroyed by blight. Since a large part of the Irish population survived on a diet consisting mainly of potatoes and buttermilk there was nothing for the starving poor to eat. In their weakened condition people had little resistance to diseases like cholera and typhus. More than one million Irish men, women, and children died of starvation during the Famine years. Many emigrated to work in the factories of the industrial cities of Liverpool and Glasgow. Many more sailed to Canada and the United States of America, from the ports of Derry and Sligo, Ballyshannon and Donegal Town.

OUR FAMILY'S DANISH ANCESTORS ON BORNHOLM

INTRODUCTION

A wealth of Danish records, variously covering from the 1500's onward including Bornholm, is now becoming available on-line.

Recently Jens Wichmann Hansen, working with the original, pre 1814, handwritten, Gothic Script, church records for all the Bornholm parishes, has produced a database that is now available via the Internet as an aid to Bornholm genealogy and local history.

A manuscript record was made by Kr. Kure (1876-1953) for each farm on Bornholm. It lists chronologically each of the owners or occupiers or takeovers of the farm as well as land transfer tax paid and who bought or inherited from whom. It also includes information on the farm owner's parents and their whereabouts as well as birth, birthplace, marriage and death dates. At this time this database is being updated by the Bornholm Family and Local History Society.

Transcripts of Bornholm Probates from 1681-1761 include the whole island but the 1761-1860s records were organized into four record groups by district listed under each parish. There are records from 1736 to 1920 of court proceedings by Rønne City court and Land mortgages and deeds dating from 1678-1892 and there are Citizenship Lists for the towns of Rønne 1701-1891, Allinge/Sandvig 1706-1804, Neksø 1741-1859 and Hasle 1862-1925 and the census records for Bornholm from 1787 and 1845 are complete.

This now accessible information has made it easier to access our Bornholm side of the family tree and has revealed several illustrious ancestors as well as the ordinary every-day man and woman.

I owe a debt of gratitude to Bjarne A. Kofoed of DK-8732 Hovedgård. He has compiled a database containing over 6000 Bornholm ancestors. After I contacted him he used his database and sent me a 159 page document with all the ancestors he could find for our grandfather Jørgen Michael Larsen Wandahl.

THE ISLAND OF BORNHOLM

The rolling, heather-covered hills of this small granite island are covered  with a patchwork of farms, green and fertile fields, traditional, picturesque villages and beautiful forests. The coastline is graced by powder-white, sandy beaches and rocky cliffs that frame fishing villages. Its present tranquillity belies a turbulent past. It was through these turbulent centuries that our ancestors were born, lived worked, married and died on this small island of approximately 600 square kilometres (230 square miles). Though located only 40 kilometres southeast of the southern tip of Sweden in the Baltic Sea, the island is territorially part of Denmark.

Hampered by a strategically important position, Bornholm (holm is the Danish word for island), has constantly struggled to defend itself from invasion, plundering pirates and the medieval struggle between royal and religious forces.

Living on Bornholm was never easy and, over the years, the populace suffered foreign domination as Denmark struggled to secure its sovereignty and independence from the larger, stronger military forces that surrounded it on every side.

Before AD 1000 Bornholm was inhabited by Vikings[13]. Over the centuries it belonged, in turn, to Denmark, the Hanseatic League, Lübeck, and Sweden. In 1658 a group of revolutionaries shot the Swedish Commandant Printzensköld and freed Bornholm. In 1660, the island reverted to Danish control. In 1806, during the Napoleonic wars, the British bombed Copenhagen. In 1807 the Danish state became bankrupt. In the war of 1864, Denmark lost Norway to Sweden and shortly after that, huge parts of Jutland were lost to Germany.

In 1427, the Hanseatic League plundered the island of Bornholm and other Danish islands. A hundred years later between 1525 and 1575, the Hanseatic League dominated trading between Europe and Britain and the people of Bornholm were suppressed with high taxes and forced work. German merchants and mercenaries from Lübeck ruled the island of Bornholm. From approximately 1650-1750 most of the Danish administration positions and top military posts were occupied by Germans of noble birth. Several of our ancestors belonged to this group and several of those were not born on Bornholm itself.

At this present time, in the year 2012, I would point out that since our grandfather Jørgen Michael Larsen Wandahl[14] was born in1867 three generations of the Vandal family presently cover a total of 144 years.

---

[13] The Norsemen came from the three countries of Scandinavia: Denmark, Norway and Sweden. Those who left Scandinavia and went off raiding in longships were said to be 'going Viking' i.e. 'going on a pirate raid'.

Some went to fight and pillage but most of those 'going Viking' were fishers, hunters, skilled craftsmen or farmers who, because of poor quality home land, sailed overseas to search for good farming land to make a better life for their family. They settled in new lands as farmers, craftsmen or traders and established trade and trade routes in their quest to gain material wealth.

[14] In old documents the name was always spelt Wandahl and in later documents Vandahl, a place name meaning Waterdale or Watervalley. Since such a place does not exist on Bornholm a more logical explanation could be that Wandahl, (in Danish w and v are the some sounds) was possibly a nickname that was enhanced with the letters "w" and "h" to make it look better when priests recorded family marriages, baptisms and burials.

His father Hans Larsen Wandahl Fischer, born 1829 would be our great grandfather and his grandfather Lars Mortensen Wandahl, born 1792 would be our 2 times great grandfather. I only mention this in case anyone thinks that the number of greats and the dates do not tie in correctly with each other.

Our Family's German
Ancestors on Bornholm

Lieutenant-Colonel Julius Erick von Fischer (1645), our 6 times great grandfather, was the son of a distinguished noble family from Lüneburg[15] and was Commandant on Bornholm from 1676 to 1680. His wife, Anne Cathrine Diderichsdatter von Busch, (1647 – 1715) our 6 times great grandmother, was the daughter of Colonel Dietrich von Busch (1619) from the principality of Jülich[16], Tyskland and Anne Ketler von Kleve (1620). Although Anne Cathrine Diderichsdatter von Busch was born at Malmø, Skåne the family were not Swedish. She died in 1715 at 15 vg St Kannikegård, Bodilsker.

Our 5 times great grandfather Captain Hans Mathias Juliusen von Fischer, born 1665 at Jylland, was the son of Lieutenant-Colonel Julius Erick von Fischer, and his wife, Anne Cathrine Diderichsdatter von Busch. At a time when the countries of Europe were in a state of almost continuous warfare (separately and in varying and shifting coalitions) with each other, Mathias served firstly as a military officer in the von Rathlaus Dragon Corps then continued on to Prince Christian's Regiment in 1683. He was promoted

---

[15]   The city of Lüneburg is located between Hamburg and Hanover in Lower Saxony. It is mentioned in the records for the first time in the year 956 in connection with the salt works. Its merchants were founder members of the Hanseatic League and the splendid gables of the buildings show the former fortune of the city.

[16]   Jülich is a medium-sized town in the district Dueren, in the state of North Rhine-Westphalia in Germany, not far from Aachen

to Second Lieutenant in 1686. He fought in Ireland as part of the English coalition army of William III.[17]

Mathias was promoted as Lieutenant July 28th, 1691 in Prince Christian's regiment. By November 10th, 1695 he was promoted to Captain in The Danish Battalion in which he served until he returned to Denmark after the 1697 peace of Risjwick in Holland. He then served with the second Battalion in Brabant. After the Battle of Høschelt, August 13th, 1704, he so mentally affected by all that he had endured that he became long-term sick. His resignation from the field was accepted in January 7th, 1705. From August 12th, 1705 until November 12th, 1724 he served as captain of a volunteer company on Christiansø. In 1706 he married Charlotte Louise Amelia Mathiasdatter von Echstein

Charlotte Louise Hansdatter von Fischer (1706 - 1789), our 4 times great grandmother, was born circa 1706. She married, on October 22nd, 1738, Casper Andersen Kamper at Nexø Kirke and then, on 26th, Nov 1749, Rasmus Rasmussen Brand also at Nexø Kirke. In 1789 she died at Nexø. Her parents were Hans Mathias Juliusen von Fischer (1665), Charlotte Louise Amelia Mathiasdatter von Echstein (1671).

---

[17]   On June 14th, 1690, the Protestant King William III entered Ireland at the head of an army consisting of a coalition of Danish, French, Dutch, and Huguenot, German, English and even Irish troops. Waiting to meet him was the army loyal to the deposed Roman Catholic King James VII of Scotland and II of England. Each of these armies was led by a man who insisted that he, and only he, was the rightful King of Britain.

On July 1st, 1690 the two armies met on the banks of the River Boyne. It was not a battle of Protestants against Roman Catholics, political issues were far more important and the Protestant William actually had the support of Pope Innocent XI and European allies drawn from the League of Augsburg - an anti-French coalition of nobility that included Roman Catholic states as well.

One reason why this battle achieved so much fame (or infamy) was that it was the only time both kings, William III and James II, were actually on a battlefield, facing each other (albeit at a distance). Irish issues were never really raised. It wasn't even about Ireland - yet it became one of the most iconic events in Irish history.

Despite its ultimate historical insignificance in Irish history, the Battle of the Boyne still to this day raises antagonistic reactions from many of the Roman Catholic faith.

Dietrich von Busch (1619 - 1677), our 7 times great grandfather, was born circa 1619 at Tyskland (Germany) He married Anne Ketler von Kleve circa 1639. His daughters were born at Malmø, Skåne. He died June 25th, 1677 at Malmø, Skåne. His wife, Anne Ketler von Kleve (1620 - ????), our 7 times great grandmother, was born circa 1620 at Kleve[18], Tyskland.

Mathias Michelsen von Echstein (1651 - 1678), our 6 times great grandfather, was born circa 1651 at Rosengården, Rønne. Circa 1671, he married Anne Marie Willers who was born in

Holland 1652. His parents were Michel von Echstein Ehrensegg (1626 – 1673) and Agnethe von Mühlern (1628).

Lieutenant Colonel Michael von Echstein von Ehrensegg (1626 – 1673) our 7 times great grandfather was the Commandant on Bornholm between 1658 and 1662. [It is believed he was a descendant of the Austrian noble family von Eckstein – Ehrenegg who were ennobled in 1616.] Between the years 1651–1666, he leased Simblegård. He then owned Rosengården and latterly Amtsgård in Rønne, where he died 10th, March 1673. He was buried, 26th, March 1673, in a vault under the chancel of St Clement's Kirke. His estate was valued at 4,417 dollars, a large fortune at that time.

---

[18]   Kleve, historically known in English as Cleves, is a town in the northwest of North Rhine-Westphalia in Germany, near the Dutch border and the River Rhine.

OUR FAMILY'S SCOTTISH
ANCESTORS ON BORNHOLM

Another of our ancestors was Alexander Dick (1571 - 1612) our 10 times great grandfather. He was born in Dysart, Scotland and is known on Bornholm as Sander Dich. Dysart, in the Kingdom of Fife on the East coast of Scotland, was the harbour for numerous freighters trading between Scotland and Northern Europe.

As one of the many Scottish captains engaged in the freight-trade across the North Sea and the Baltic Sea he became a well-respected merchant and one of Svåneke's most prominent citizens and as such found his last resting place beneath the church floor. His tombstone is now to be found in the graveyard leaning against the north wall.

Even before 1600, Sander Dich must have had connections to Bornholm, since records dating from 1598/99 show that Sander Skott (as he was sometimes called) was fined 9 Dalers for assaulting a Swedish captain. In the custom and duties records, Sander Dich (Skott) appears numerous times. For example in 1590: "Alexander Skott of Dundee came from Knigsberg." In 1591 he came from Danzig and again in 1596 carrying only ballast.

Karina Didrichsdatter (1575 - 1665) our 10 times great grandmother and wife of Sander Dich, has an important place in the genealogy of many Bornholm families. Not only did she become the founding mother of the branching Dich-family, but through her second marriage to ship's captain

David Wolsen also from Scotland, she is the founding mother of the Wulfsen-family of Bornholm.

Her own origins remain a mystery; she cannot be traced back either to the island's old, farm-families or to having any connections to families occupying public office on Bornholm. She is mentioned in the land-registry records as late as the early 1660's as owning land in Ibsker parish.

However, from 1667 she was no longer named in the books. The main reason that Karina Didrichsdatter's position in the Dich-family can be documented stems from the fact that Eskild Sandersen Dich's two sons, Albert and Sander Dich, in a court case in the 1670's, declared that they had inherited certain valuables from their father's mother Karina, widow of Sander Dich and also of David Wolsen.

I do not presently know from which University Haagen Sonesen (1609 - 1665), our 7 times great grandfather graduated in 1631, but from that time on he took the surname of Rønneby, that being the name of his birthplace.

Rønneby was the most important trading place in Blekinge with an excellent position about 15 km from the sea on the Rønnebyn. Haagen was the curate for Rønne-Knudsker parish in 1640 and afterwards was the pastor for Klemensker parish from 1645 until his death. The rectory burned down on Pentecostal night 1652 and unfortunately all documents and church records were destroyed.

In the early 1600's during a time of plague, Danish control of Bornholm was lost to Sweden. Swedish rule on the island was extremely harsh and people were forced to pay high taxes to the suppressive forces. In 1658, a Johan Printzensköld was appointed Commandant (Oberst) of the Swedish garrison. Not too long after this Commandant Printzensköld was "invited" to a party at the parsonage of Klemensker parish.

At that party, Haagen Rønneby and one of his daughters mistakenly let it be known that they admired the Danish king and sympathized with him. As compensation for this alleged insult the Swedish Commandant insisted that his host "give" him a silver jug and the best horse on the farm.

On December 8th, 1658 the people of Bornholm rebelled against their Swedish overlords and Commandant Johan Printzensköld was executed in Rønne and the Swedish army stationed in the fortress of Hammershus were forced to surrender. Swedish re-enforcements were captured as they landed at Sandvig during Christmas-time and the islanders freed themselves from years of foreign command. The rebellion's leaders, Jens Pedersen Kofoed (1628- 1691), Poul Anker, Peder Olsen and Villum Clausen were celebrated as champions of liberty.

Great suffering and losses caused by the European plague did not make life any easier for the islanders. From 1645 through until 1654 several waves of plague struck the Danish populace killing many thousands of people. On Bornholm the "Great Plague" of 1653-1654 killed a total of 4,895 people, probably at least a quarter of the population. In Åker[19] alone 557 people perished from the plague which raged through the island.

---

[19] The church for Åkirkeby township and Åker is located just outside of the township of Åkirkeby proper, so paradoxically enough the town that draws its name from the "River Church" (Aae Kirke) does not actually have a church within its municipal boundaries at all. Åkirkeby was the traditional seat of Bornholm's judiciary authority, its "Landsting" (Parliament), and the Aae Kirke was used as their meeting place.

Our Family's Notable Farmer Ancestors on Bornholm

A great many of our Bornholm ancestors were farmers. Several were big farmers (freemen) others were tenant farmers or small landholders. Several were rich, others were poor. However, irrespective of wealth or position they all suffered plague, wars, foreign domination, being plundered and being suppressed with high taxes.

A widow, especially of a farmer, usually had to hurry and find a new husband to take over the obligations connected with the lease. If the widow had children, then the new husband took over the management of the farm as an "opsidder" - which is a very Old Danish word used to describe a man who marries a widow who has a child who is heir to the farm. (On Bornholm the heir was usually the youngest son, and if no sons - then the eldest daughter.) When the heir reached the age of maturity, his mother and her new husband would hand over the farm to the heir; after which they would either retire or find another farm for themselves.

By tradition, once a couple's betrothal was officially announced in church, they could begin living together as man and wife. For many, marriages were formed as the result of necessity: a widowed man or woman quickly needed a new wife/husband to look after his/her children/farm. The practice of living together after announcing their betrothal allowed the couple to put off the more involved wedding ceremony, and celebration, till a more convenient time - usually 2 or 3 months later. As a result it is not uncommon to see children being born 9 months after the betrothal, rather than after the wedding.

There were three classes of farms (gård) on the island.

1] Proprietairgård (Propr.), earlier called a Friegård - meaning property owned by a "free-man" ("frimand", later called a "proprietær").

2] Selvejergård (Slg.) - meaning a farm owned independently, free of obligations to a property owner - it could be occupied by its owner or rented out to a peasant farmer (bonde).

3] Vornedegård (Vdg.), also spelled Vårnedergård - meaning a farm leased out long-term by a land-owner (proprietær) to a tenured peasant farmer; these farms were "attached" to a proprietairgård, and entailed accompanying work obligations by the peasant for the proprietår who held the rights on the farm's lease.

There was very little difference between the self-owned farmers [Selvejer; abbreviated SE, Sg. Slg.] and the serf-farmers [Vorned; abbreviated Vg, Vdg]. Vornedgård had to pay a few extra small fees. There also appears to have been the possibility of movement, depending on good or bad fortune, between the groups.

On Bornholm the farms (in Danish "gård", or old style "gaard") had long standing official names and numbers. The typical farm was arranged in a joined U shape, with the farmhouse, barn, pig-stall, and utility-shed all built around a cobble-stone courtyard. Each farm was listed by an official number, which was important for identification.

Families usually stayed in the same basic geographic region. They also tended to move together, although they were not likely to move across the country. Most of the population lived on rural farming estates. Records show that, for many years, the Wandahl family lived within the boundaries of Bodilsker Parish.

Mogens Grubbe[20] (1615 - ????) our 7 times great grandfather, owned the farm Pg Simblegård at Klemensker. The letters Pg with the farm name

---

[20] There are several mentions of the "Grubbe" surname on Bornholm during this time period. Sivert Grubbe, of Bodilsker was an Examiner (judge). Jacob Grubbe is recorded, in 1658, as being "well-born".

indicates that the property was owned by a "free-man" ("frimand", later called a "proprietær"). It is believed that the Grubbe family, who were regarded as Danish nobility, first lived at Simblegård circa 1500.

Shortly after 1625, Hans Nielsen (1600 - 1689) our 9 times great grandfather lived at one of the four farms known collectively as the "Risby-farms". His farm was burned down by the Swedes during war-time in 1645. It is recorded that in the middle of the night the Swedish cavalry broke down the doors of the farm and dragged a woman out of her childbirth-bed whilst the owner, Hans Nielsen, hid in the hay. The Swedish Captain set fire to everything, including all the harvested grain. It is also recorded that because of the destruction King Christian IV freely gave building-timber from his forests to rebuild Risby farm.

Pilegård is one of the oldest-recognized, owner's name for a farm where, at the end of the 1500's and in the first decade of the 1600's, Jens Jespersen (c1550 - c1610) our 9 times great grandfather is recorded as being the owner.

Rasmus Laursen (1575 - 1605), our 8 times great grandfather, owned three farms. By 1598 he had acquired Rågelundsgård, 8' Slg. in Rø parish. The other two, Bakkegård, 21' Slg. and Skovgård, 22' Slg. are in Rutsker parish.

In 1651, Hans Jensen (1620 - 1678) our 7 times great grandfather, leased Tyndekuldegård (also spelled Tøndekullegård) from Mogens Christensen, paying him 210 Silverdalers for the privilege. He lived, with his wife Karen Hansdatter, (1621 1678) our 7 times great grandmother, and farmed there for 20 years after which time the lease was renewed. In 1673 Hans Jensen leased the neighbouring farm Kyrkkegård, 14 Slg. for 16 years, from Lars Larsen for the sum of 80 Silverdalers; it had been devastated by a fire.

By February 23, 1678 both Hans Jensen and his wife Karen, were dead and inheritance proceedings took place. On Bornholm the youngest son normally took over father's lease, paying off the other heirs. The couple left eight children, but none of them were especially eager to take over the lease of the farm, valued at 210 Silverdalers, so it was agreed that the eldest son, 36 year old Peder Hansen could get it for 140 Silverdalers.

In 1625, Hans Low (1600 - 1647) our 6 times great grandfather, obtained Tornegård, 34' Slg. Åker. Its "official" name was Tornegård however after Hans Low purchased the farm it was known locally as "Lauegård" (Low's farm). The Low family owned the farm for several generations before it passed into Kofoed family ownership.

His wife, Karen Hansdatter (1615 - 1654) our 6 times great grandmother is believed to have died of the plague which ravaged Bornholm 1653- 54.

The family name of this branch of our tree has been variously spelled: Low, Lov, Loug, Lou, and Lau. Hans Low's original place of birth is not known, nor who his parents were, but because there is a Lau family in southern Jylland (Duchies of Schleswig and Holstein) it has been suggested that the family has its ancient roots in northern Germany.

Anders Larsen (1664 - 1740), another of our 5 times great grandfathers was the second of seven sons. He married Helvig Haagensdatter (1655 - 1729), daughter of Haagen Sonesen Rønneby (1609 - 1665) and our 5 times great grandmother. They lived on Brogård, 30' Slg. Åker.

After his marriage to Helvig, Anders was able to pay off the creditors to his family-farm of Boesgård.

The total purchase price was 220 Silverdalers and on March 1, 1700, he paid to his father Lars Hansen the sum of 50 Silverdalers, so that now he no longer had "any part or parcel of Boesgård, 46' Slg. in Klemensker". However he is recorded as being the owner of Boesgård from 1698 until 1719, at which time he sold it to his brother Peder Larsen.

OUR FAMILY'S LESS NOTABLE FARMER ANCESTORS ON BORNHOLM

It would appear that one or two of our ancestors bordered on being regarded as less than reputable. It is recorded that Anders Mogensen (1663 - 1734), our 5 times great grandfather who farmed at 20 Sg. Klemensker hanged himself in the porch of Klemensker's Church.

Michel Hansen (1769 - 1812), our 2 times great grandfather was not born on Bornholm. From historical records it would appear that he was from the island of Sjælland, and that he was sent to Bornholm because "he was not behaving himself well". Since his birth place on Sjælland is not recorded it has not been possible to find his christening record nor the names of his parents.

The move seems to have achieved its purpose and on 01 December 1792 he and Elisabeth Kirstine Hansdatter Low were married at Å Kirke, Åker. They had 9 children. He named his eldest son Hans Nielsen Michelsen Low, so it seems possible, since Danish surnames tended to follow a patronymic system and the first son was traditionally named after the paternal grandfather, that Michel's father's name was Hans Nielsen. Michel Hansen later took his wife's family name of Low.

The Åker registry records that before his marriage, Corporal Hans Poulsen Low (1724 - 1794) our three times great grandfather, was having personal and financial difficulties. There are also entries made over the years concerning admonishments made to him and his wife Elisabeth/Lisabeth Larsdatter for their very public display of their personal problems.

Great tragedy in the family life of Hans and Lisabeth was a contributing factor to their problems; only one of their five children survived childhood. The youngest son Poul was only 40 days old when he died of smallpox.

In the November of 1757, Hans' parents both died and were buried on the same day in Åker. As the only boy to survive his parents Hans Lov received the inheritance rights to 34' Slg. Lauegård in Åker. On several occasions, it is recorded that Hans was publicly and severely admonished from the pulpit for his continuously deplorable way of life, and constant drunkenness. He supposedly gambled and drank Lauegård away, slowly selling off parts of the land to pay his debts.

As was customary, his five sisters did not immediately receive their inheritance which was left standing in the farm however three of his brothers-in-law lost their homes and all belongings in the great fire in Åkirkeby on May 10th 1760.

The disaster forced them to claim their wives' inheritance and this made Hans' economic difficulties much worse. He was not able to pay them without mortgaging the farm which he finally had to sell in 1761. The family then lived in Rønne for several years, after which they moved back to Åker.

Our ancestors on Bornholm were certainly a diverse group of people from virtually every strata of society from its "underachievers" to its high flyers. It is not known how much Grandpa Vandal knew of his family history but he certainly must have been aware of some of his relatives at the very least his uncles, aunts, cousins and grandparents.

Grandpa Vandal

Grandpa Vandal's father was Hans Larsen Fischer Vandal (1829 - ????) our great grandfather who was born at Bodilsker. Grandpa's mother was Johanne Cathrine (Andersdatter)[21] Jørgensen, our great grandmother who was born in 1831 at 38 sg grund, Åker.

The name Fischer probably comes from Lieutenant-Colonel Julius Erick von Fischer (1645), our 6 times great grandfather but I am unable to confirm this. I still have not been able to trace the origins of the name Vandahl though it is possibly a place name.

All of the children of Hans Larsen had the name Larsen as well as Vandahl. Hans Jorgen Larsen Vandal was born 1858, Johannes Christian Larsen Vandal, was born 1860, Poul Thorius Larsen Vandal, was born 1862, Mouritz Peter Larsen Vandal, was born 1865 and Jørgen Michel Larsen Vandal (Grandpa Vandal), was born 1867. Circa 1880 he seems to disappear from the Bornholm records. In Scotland Grandpa Vandal used the name George, the English language form of Jørgen.

Grandpa Vandal was the youngest of the family and was presumably, according to the custom on Bornholm, in line to eventually inherit his

---

[21] Until the mid-1800s, Danish surnames followed a patronymic system. A father's given name was typically used for his children's surname. For example, Lars Mortensen's children had the surname Larsen (son of Lars) or Larsdatter (daughter of Lars). Peder Larsen, Lars' son, gave his children the surname of Pedersen (male) or Pedersdatter (female). By the mid-1800s this naming pattern was phased out, and one surname was passed through succeeding generations. Wandahl (Vandahl) became the dominant surname for our family.

father's lease of the farm and pay off the other heirs. This may have been one reason why he ran away and may also have given rise to the story that he wanted to go to sea and the family were against it. Anyway at this late stage there is no way of proving all of this but I find it an interesting theory.

GRANDPA VANDAL AND GRANNY VANDAL

Nothing appears to be now known about his travels and his life in the intervening years until, as Carl Larsen Vandal (Ship Steward) he married Isabella Jemmott (McConnachie) in 1893. The few Scottish records that exist for Grandpa Vandal give only a bare history

He is recorded as George Vandal but appears to be in three different places in the Scottish 1901 census. Firstly He is recorded as living at 4, Duff Street, Greenock with his wife Bella, his daughter Mary (12) and four children, George (6), Robert (4), James (2), his newly born baby Johanne and a lodger, James Fleming, who was a widower and a boatman.

Intriguingly, in this census, it would appear that he and the children are recorded as speaking Gaelic and English. This cannot now be proved one way or another but it is just possible because he was a Clyde Puffer skipper and would be constantly in contact the Gaelic speakers of the West Coast. He is not recorded in the 'If Working at Home Column' but he is recorded, under the appropriate columns as being a 'boatman' and a 'worker' (not, at this time, as an 'employer').

Secondly It would appear that at the time of the 1901 census he and two of his crew were alongside the Kames Gunpowder Wharf on Loch Fyne. At Kilfinan, George Vandal is recorded as having been born in Denmark and at the age of 34 being the master (but neither employer nor owner) of a Clyde puffer called the "Electric Light". Thirdly He was also recorded as being in the village of Kames however that entry was scored out.

In the 1901 census Elizabeth, his stepdaughter, is not with the rest of the family though her sister Mary is. It is believed that Elizabeth (Aunt Lizzie) was brought up by a relative in Greenock and using the fact that her son Charles (Chas) visited a Granny Watts, I found in the 1901 census a record of a Lizzie Watts (11years of age, born in Greenock) and a Mary Watts (a 54 year old widow, born in Ireland) as living at 5, Hamilton Street, Greenock.

Since Elizabeth (Aunt Lizzie) was born in 1890 the age of Lizzie 'Watts' is correct. One unusual fact is that the census record of 1901 records Mary Watts as being a widow but the death record for her husband Robert Watts is dated 1910. The address in both records is 5, Hamilton Street, Greenock. However, that census record has the following inscription, "This schedule was lost and a fresh one made out". It could be taken that the new schedule was less than accurate.

Hamilton Street early 1900's

Checking backwards I found a marriage record, dated 1874, for a Mary Dinan (27) to a Robert Charles Watts (24), a tugboat seaman. The addresses given were 57 and 51, Shaw Street respectively. There is a death record dated 1881, for their son Robert Watts aged 6 days. The address is also Shaw Street Greenock. Granny Vandal's daughter Elizabeth Jemmott (Aunt Lizzie) was born in 1890 at 50 Shaw Street.

Joan Catherine Vandal, the baby girl born in 1895 at 1, Smith Lane, died at the age of 4 months at 27, Hamilton Street. Joan Catherine was baptised on 5th November in St. Mary's Catholic Church, Greenock. A son, <u>Robert Charles Watts</u> Vandal, was born on 27th January 1897. When he was baptised on 5th February, 1898 in St. Mary's Catholic Church, Greenock, Mary Watts was the sponsor. It is fairly certain that Robert was named after Mary Watt's husband, Robert Charles Watts.

Since the two families, the Watts and the Vandals had lived in the same streets and since it was common practice to name children after relatives it is a reasonable assumption that the families were possibly related or at the very least knew each other extremely well.

Other records help to corroborate this assumption. In 1894 a Robert Watts was a witness at the wedding of Grandpa and Granny Vandal. However, the information in these same records also appears to suggest that these Watts were not related to the family of James Watt, the famous engineer, despite the family story that there was a family connection.

In 1899 a son, James Fleming Vandal was born at 4 Duff Street, Greenock and in1900 a daughter, Joan Fisher Vandal was also born there.

Cathcart Street looking east

The 1901 census also records that the family lived at 4 Duff Street but by August 1901 when the child Joan Fisher Vandal died at the age of 8 months, the family had moved to 16, Cathcart Street where in 1902, a son, Samuel Stewart Vandal was born and a year later in 1903, a daughter, Isabella Vandal was born.

By 1904, the family had moved once again, this time to 49 Rue End Street where a son, William Stewart Vandal was born followed in 1906 by a daughter, Margaret Anders Vandal who died at the age of 8 months.

Two sad items that appear to show that at least the family finances had improved are the following intimations that were placed in the Greenock local newspaper.

VANDAL Joan Fisher, infant daughter of George and Isabella Vandal, died at 16 Cathcart Street, Greenock on 23rd August 1901 age 8 months. (Greenock Telegraph 23.8.1901)

VANDAL Daughter to Mr & Mrs G. Vandal, born at 49 Rue-End Street, Greenock on 10th Jan 1906. (Greenock Telegraph 11.1.1906) Margaret Anders died 6th Sept 1906. (Greenock Telegraph 7.9.1906)

Sometime between 1906 and 1908 the family moved from Greenock to Paisley. It is not known why this move took place but they are recorded as living at 15, Moss Street, Paisley where, in 1908, a son, Andrew Vandal was born. However on July 12th of that year William Vandal died aged 3 years old and then on January of 1909 Andrew Vandal died aged 8 months.

The deaths of two children at 15, Moss Street must have had an impact on the family because by August 1909 when Allan McAlpine Vandal, the youngest of the family (and my father), was born the family were living in a much larger house at 3, New Sneddon Street. This address is recorded on the birth certificate.

The 1911 census records 3, New Sneddon Street as a common lodging house that Granny Vandal ran on her own account. The census further records that she was aged 43 years old; had been married for 26 years and had had 14 children of whom 8 were still living.

Mary (my aunt) (aged 22) is recorded as working in the printing department of a carpet factory and George (my uncle) (aged 16) is employed as an apprentice carpenter in the shipyard. Robert (aged 14), James (aged 12) Samuel (aged 10) and Isabella (aged 8) are recorded as scholars and Allan, the baby, is aged 1.

The Paisley trades/street directory for 1913 (in this case showing the lodging house) omits 3, New Sneddon Street completely but indicates that the family had moved to 10, New Sneddon Street, however the trades/street directory for 1914 does not mention the family as staying in New Sneddon Street.

I was hoping for information on Grandpa Vandal but he must have been on board the boat because, in the 1911 census, there appears to be no record of him or his whereabouts.

In the 1911 census Lizzie (my aunt) (aged 21) is recorded under her own surname of Jemmott and is a boarder at 5 Hamilton Street, Greenock with Mary Watts (aged 65). She is employed as a Lithographer in a cooperage.

An "all parishes" search of the Valuation Roll of 1915 shows only ONE record for the name Vandal, George Vandal Jr., Boatman, was a tenant at 20, Underwood Lane[22] at a rent of £7.6s.0d per year (2/9d per week). The inclusion of what appears to be the letters Jr. (junior) after the name raises a presently unanswerable query. It suggests that the tenant was not Grandpa Vandal but his son George.

A similar all parishes search of the Valuation Roll of 1915 for Robert Stevenson, (Grandpa Stevenson) produced 242 matches. However in a refined Paisley parishes search he is recorded as being a tenant at 19, Underwood Lane at a rent of £10 per year (3/9d per week).

The marriage record in 1921 for Samuel Vandal gives the address as 20, Underwood Lane but the marriage record in 1931 of Allan McAlpine Vandal gives the address as 28, Underwood Lane.

Of the eleven children born to Granny Vandal and Grandpa Vandal five died at a young age and during World War I, Robert Charles Watts Vandal, aged 20, joined the 11th (Service) Battalion Princess Louise's (Argyll and Sutherland Highlanders).

He was killed in action at the Battle at Arras 23rd April 1917.[23] (The British took the village of Guemappe but little else on the 23rd April and on one day suffered 10,000 casualties. During the Great War a total of 431 officers and 6,475 other ranks of the Argyll & Sutherland Highlanders' lost their lives and six Victoria Crosses were awarded to the regiment.)

---

[22] This was a street of four-storey, grey sandstone, tenement blocks that housed 12 artisan families in flats (houses) accessed from a central, communal stairway. The yearly rent for individual flats indicated the size (number/size of rooms) of the accommodation, a "single end" (a one room flat) being the cheapest.

[23]

Name	Rank	Service Number	Date of Death	Age	Regiment / Service	Service Country	Grave / Memorial Reference	Cemetery / Memorial Name
VANDAL, ROBERT	Private	S/43226	23/04/1917	20	Argyll and Sutherland Highlanders	United Kingdom	20. A. 15.	CANADIAN CEMETERY NO.2. NEUVILLE-ST. VAAST

He was buried (in the Canadian Cemetery No. 2, in Neuville-St Vaast, Pas de Calais, France.

Accessing modern records of living people is not so easy therefore the following information is, I believe, as accurate as I can make it though I would be happy to receive any corrections.

As well as Mary and Elizabeth (Lizzie), the daughters of Granny Vandal's first marriage, there were five children who survived into adulthood; George Larsen Vandal, James Fleming Vandal, Samuel Stewart Vandal (who died in 1942), Isabella Vandal and Allan McAlpine Vandal. George Vandal and Isabella Vandal did not marry.

In 1914, Mary Adelaide Jemmott (my Aunt Mary) married Allan McAlpine. They had three sons: George Vandal McAlpine, born in 1915, Robert Vandal McAlpine born in 1918 and John McAlpine. In 1935, George married Henrietta McKellar Fudge. Their son Allan McAlpine was born in 1938. In 1942, Henrietta died of pulmonary tuberculosis.

In 1949, John McAlpine married May (Mary) Mitchell Gallacher (born Dec. 28th, 1925).

In 1950, Robert Vandal McAlpine married Catherine Calde Clements and a son, John Clements McAlpine, was born in 1954.

Robert was in the Seaforth Highlanders during W.W.II and was taken prisoner at St. Vallery when the 51st Div. became isolated in a diversionary action away from the main evacuation at Dunkirk. He was a P.O.W. in Silesia for part of the time and was repatriated in the spring of '45. John served his time as a plumber, and eventually was called-up into the R.E.M.E. fairly close to the end of the war. George had a 'reserved-occupation' during the war; he worked at Rolls Royce at Hillington in the aircraft engine factory. He took up massage and physiotherapy as a hobby..

After the war, on their demobilisation, both George and Robert became heavily involved with the Paisley Pirates Ice Hockey team. Many of the players were Canadian Service Men and when they returned home both George and Robert emigrated to Canada.

100th Birthday of Mary McAlpine (Jemmott)

Over the years their mother (my Aunt Mary) visited them in Canada and finally at the age of 95, being the last survivor of Granny Vandal's sons and daughters, she emigrated. The photograph shows her celebrating her 100th birthday on June 8th, 1988. Standing just behind her is Isa Vandal (my mother).

In 1914, Elizabeth Jemmott (my Aunt Lizzie) married John Flood in St Mary's Church, Greenock. They continued to stay in Greenock and lived near to Cartsdyke Station.

In 1924 their son Chas (Charles) was born. For many years he courted Bunty (Jessica) O'Neill whom he, at the age of 43, eventually married in 1963. They appear to have possibly had two children. The first son, Joseph Flood was born 1963 and the second, Michael James Flood, was born 1967.

In 1921, Samuel Stewart Vandal (my Uncle Sammy) married Margaret Boyd. They had ten children. James Fleming Vandal was born in 1924 and died in 2003; Samuel Stewart Vandal was born in 1926 and died in 2004; Jean Vandal was born in 1926; Isabella McConnachie Vandal was born in 1928; Margaret Boyd Vandal was born in 1924 and died in 1995.

Adelaide McAlpine Vandal was born in 1932; Annie Boyd Vandal was born in 1933; George Vandal was born in 1934; Robert Vandal was born in 1939 and William Boyd Vandal was born in 1941 Samuel Stewart Vandal (my Uncle Sammy) died in 1942.

In 1942, James Fleming Vandal (my Uncle James) married Jessie Forrest Roy, a divorcee (or widow) who lived next door at 138 Gallowhill Road, Paisley. For some reason this seemed to upset Grandpa Vandal and unfortunately for many years James and his family were ostracised and there was very little contact between the family members until after

Grandpa Vandal's death in 1949. They had two children, Iris Roy Vandal who was born in 1946 and James Fleming Vandal who was born in 1948.

In 1931, Allan McAlpine Vandal (my father) married Isabella Ramsay Stevenson (my mother). They had four children, Carl George Vandal was born in 1932; Agnes Millar Vandal was in born 1937 (in 1938, aged 1 year and 2 months, she died of measles and bronchial pneumonia); Robert Stevenson Vandal was born in 1939 and Allan Vandal was born in 1942. In 2000 Allan died, in Scarborough, of cancer of the palette.

Though there are family stories that Grandpa Vandal owned at least one (though possibly two) Clyde Puffer called the "X" I have not as yet been able to confirm this. Dan McDonald, on page 10 of his book "The Clyde Puffer", writes about the various owners of Clyde Puffers. Owners were numerous as the price of second hand vessels was not beyond the means of a small-business man.

X	Y
Built by Scotts of Bowling, Yard No 45	Built by Scotts of Bowling, Yard No 44
Propulsion: steam screw 11nhp	Propulsion: steam screw 11nhp
Built: 1882	Built: 1882
Ship Type: Lighter	Ship Type: Lighter
Tonnage: 71grt 42net	Tonnage: 71grt 42net
Length: 66.0ft	Length: 66.0ft
Breadth: 17.7ft	Breadth: 17.7ft
Owner History:	Owner History:
- James Currie & Co, Leith	- James Currie & Co, Leith
- 19xx Neptune Marine Salvage Co Ltd, Glasgow	- 19xx Smith & Watt Ltd, Dunfermline

The "X" was originally built for Currie's Leith, Hull & Hamburg Steam Packet Company. All their puffers had letters of the alphabet for names. McDonald also writes, on page 11 of his book that James Currie & Company sold three of their puffers to Clyde owners but he does not record which puffers were sold or who became the new owners.

I was certainly aware of the family story that during the depression[24] of the 1930's Grandpa Vandal had said, 'Why should I employ men when my own sons are out of work?' and that he had employed his sons as crew on

---

[24] In 1929, the Wall Street Crash plunged the USA into economic chaos and this created a depression across the rest of the world. In Northern Ireland, Scotland, Wales and the north of England, the coal mines, steel works and shipyards closed. In all these areas of heavy industry that employed large numbers of workers, almost every single man in the area was made redundant.

Puffers lying at Paisley Harbour

his puffer. I also remember seeing the puffer 'X' lying abandoned in Paisley Harbour and remember being told that it had been owned by Grandpa Vandal.

In the 1940's it was the accepted practice for all the family to visit, on Saturday evening, Grandpa Vandal at 138, Gallowhill Road. The hall-way at Grandpa's house in Gallowhill was long and dark and poorly lit because the bulb might have been low wattage. I thought that I remembered that a large rocking horse stood in the hallway at Gallowhill but my brother Carl tells me that the rocking horse was in Aunt Mary's hallway at Barterholm. He used to always give it a good workout when he was younger, and thinks that by the time my brother Allan and I were taken to visit her she probably banned its use for the sake of peace and quiet.

Since, during the early years of the 40's the men were involved either as soldiers or in other war work, these gatherings mainly consisted of the aunts and cousins.

At a certain time during the evening we all had to sit quietly to listen to 'The McFlannels'. In the 1940's and 50's a radio serial, The McFlannels, (Glasgow's very own soap opera about a family of working-class characters), was very popular. They never did anything wrong. The story-lines contained no bad language ever, no violence and no hint ever of a sexual scandal. It was all good, clean, wholesome fun and a good night's listening.

The closest the programmes came to a crime was when Mrs McTweed sent for the "polis" because she believed Mrs McFlannel had stolen her door mat only to discover that it was the "weans" who, for a bit of innocent fun, had simply hidden it. The radio was a sizeable (and expensive) piece of furniture. These visits stopped after Grandpa Vandal died in 1949 though my Aunt Isa and her brother, my Uncle George continued to live there until they died.

There does not appear to be any concrete evidence that Grandpa and Granny Vandal inherited property or money from family or anyone else but what is more probable is that any wealth they did manage to accumulate came from their own hard work.

Entrance to the Astoria Cinema

On the day of Grandpa Vandal's funeral (since 'children did not attend funerals') my younger brother, Allan, and I were sent to the cinema. I can remember standing on the pavement in a queue at the entrance gates to the Astoria Cinema (nick-named the Bug Hut) in Lawn Street, Paisley and wondering if it was my grandfather's funeral cortège that passed along the street.

When the gates were opened there was a longish walk along a path between two overgrown patches of land. On the left hand patch, just inside the gate, there was a derelict, rusty, horse-drawn, circus animal cage. Though the admission price was cheaper than the other town cinemas it was patronised less on wet days because the queue had to stand in the open waiting for the doors to open.

I had always wondered why the seating in that cinema was all on the flat. It was only recently that I discovered that in the early 1900's the building had been an ice rink therefore the flat floor and no balconies.

A note on the Clyde Puffers

Since the 1901 census records the names of three people (one of them being George Vandal) on the boat at Kilfinan it would imply that the Electriclight was either a shorehead boat or was shorthanded and since the company Ross & Marshall were established in 1872 and from early days adopted names ending in 'light', which reflected the name of the owning company, The Light Shipping Co., Ltd., it would suggest that the puffer belonged to that company. In 1920 they certainly had in their fleet a puffer called Electriclight. On the demise of that company it would appear that their records were acquired by Glasgow University.

The puffer was a descendant of two vessels, the scow (a canal boat narrow enough for the canal locks) and the gabbart (a small, one-masted, sloop-rigged, sailing vessel used for coastal trading).

The canal boats worked mostly on the Forth and Clyde canal and the upper reaches of the River Clyde. The 'shorehead' boats, i.e. the estuary boats, had a crew of three; measured up to 66' in length by 15' to 16' beam with a loaded draught of up to 7', and carried a cargo up to 80 tons.

The 'outside' boats, i.e. the sea-going coasters, had a crew of four including a deckhand; were 66' in length by up to 18'6" beam with a loaded draught

of 9'6", the limit for The Crinan Canal, and carried a maximum cargo of 120 tons. (N.B the symbol 'used after a number indicates feet and the symbol" used after a number indicates inches therefore 9'6" means a length of 9 feet 6 inches which is very approximately two metres).

stowing the dingy[25]

stowing the dingy[25]

These coastal vessels were powered by a coal-fired, non-condensing, steam engine. After the steam had activated the piston in the single cylinder, it was exhausted up the funnel. When combined with the black smoke from the coal furnace, these repeated "puffs" gave the ships their famous name. Derricks were fitted, not always with a steam winch, for cargo work and for putting a man ashore to work locks and drawbridges on the canal. To go under Glasgow bridges their masts lowered onto a tabernacle.

Being a crew member on a puffer was not an easy life. As well as sailing the boat in all but the roughest of weathers they very often had to physically load and unload the cargo.

Board of Trade Certificates were few and far between but what was more

important was that the skippers were all resourceful seamen with many years of sailing experience and with a good knowledge of the coast especially as it was often necessary to deliver cargoes to destinations that had no harbour. With a nearly flat bottom the puffer was able to

---

[25] In this photograph, from page 22 of Dan McDonald's book 'The Clyde Puffer', the person operating the winch is my father, Allan Vandal, youngest son of the family.

be beached at high tide, unloaded at low tide and floated off with the following high tide. Many skippers had progressed from the position of engineman so they knew also something about engines. The deckhand was usually cook and relief engineer as well.

A note on the Kames Gunpowder Works

The Kames Gunpowder Works at Millhouse and Kames commenced production in 1839 and continued until 1921. The mainly Gaelic speaking population of the parish numbered about 1,820 people.

The gunpowder was packed into bags and barrels or boxes, ready for dispatch. The bags were sewn on site. As a safety precaution, all the girls had to wear navy blue overalls with caps to match. They were not allowed any metal hairpins. For the same reason, their shoes were soled with copper nails. They had to provide their own food as well as soap and towels for washing after work. Only one small tub of hot water per person was provided by the company. More than twenty girls were employed at different periods in the Packing Department.

All the male process workers had to wear moleskin trousers without pockets. Like the girls in the Packing House, they were issued with special boots soled with copper nails. To avoid the danger of causing sparks which could result in an explosion all implements were made from brass, bronze, copper or wood. Shovels were wooden and riddles had copper mesh.

Before starting each shift, they were searched thoroughly. Pipe smokers were allowed to chew tobacco. Despite the obvious danger to themselves and their workmates, some men hid clay pipes and matches in the joints of the boundary wall.

Many employees walked several miles to and from Millhouse daily. Those who came from crofts which had no road access carried candles in jam jars to light their way across the hills in winter.

The essential requirements for the location of a gunpowder works were: - (a) to be remote from towns or cities to minimise damage from explosions, (b) to have easy access to the sea for receiving raw materials and dispatching finished products, (c) to have a reliable water supply to drive the machinery and (d) to have the availability of male and female workforce. The villages of Millhouse and Kames satisfied all these criteria.

The Kames Gunpowder Company, which was taken over by Curtis and Harvey in 1876, had its own pier at Kames, on the Kyles of Bute, where supplies of the required raw materials were unloaded. In the early days, some of these incoming cargoes were carried by sailing ships. However, in later years the trade was taken over by "puffers", bearing names such as Moonlight, Starlight, Skylight and Twilight.

Much of the gunpowder that was produced at Millhouse was exported overseas, so schooners, deep sea sailing vessels, had to be used. All these ships had to fly the international symbol, a red flag, to show they were carrying or were loading explosives. When they arrived at Kames, carrying ballast of coal, they were either anchored or were moored to a large buoy near the Bute shore.

The cargoes of gunpowder barrels and boxes had to be ferried to and from the pier at Kames in small boats (the puffers). It has been suggested that schooners were used for shipping the gunpowder since they were originally built entirely of wood and used sail for propulsion and were therefore considered to be safer than iron steamships with their coal-fired boilers.

Our Family's Maternal Ancestors in Scotland in the 19th Century

INTRODUCTION

In the 19th Century, the economic and social structure of Scotland changed dramatically. Over two-thirds of the population still lived and worked on the land, or in small industrial villages. They had a hard but tolerable standard of living. The only exception was in the Highlands where the people were almost universally poverty stricken.

Looking for work and accommodation, large numbers of migrants from the Highlands (forced out to make room for sheep) and from Ireland, crowded into the growing cities of Glasgow and Dundee.

This sudden influx of impoverished migrants from the Highlands and Ireland created massive accommodation and environmental problems and it was cities such as Glasgow and Dundee that experienced the worst incidences of overcrowding, disease and poverty.

Transport was on foot or by horse and cart along makeshift roads, or by canal or river in wooden barges and ships. There was no rail link between Edinburgh and Glasgow until 1842.

In the first half of the 19th century, daily life, with its shift from agriculture to industry and its working day of 14 to 16 hours, was monotonous and routine for most of the population.

However, by the mid-1840's the growth of the iron industry, in the Central Belt of Lowland Scotland, close to the Lanarkshire coalfields and with the introduction of iron shipbuilding and marine engineering there was a demand for greater efficiency in the coal industry.

Wages increased, the standard of living improved and a larger number of Scots began to enjoy a greater prosperity and a more respectable and varied lifestyle. It was in this rapidly changing world that our Scottish ancestors lived and, by dint of personal determination and hard work, prospered.

OUR FAMILY'S ANCESTORS FROM THE SCOTTISH ISLAND OF ISLAY

GRAN STEVENSON

Islay (Islay, pronounced Eye-la, is the anglicised spelling; in Gaelic the island is still spelt Ile.) was originally divided up into six parishes; Kildalton; Oa; Kilmeny; Portnahaven; Bowmore (or Kilarrow); Kilchoman.[26]

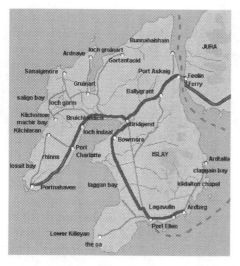

Prior to 1855, when statutory Registration of Births, Deaths and Marriages became compulsory, parish registers were kept. These registers were maintained by the Church of Scotland and cover baptism or births, proclamation of banns or marriages and burials or deaths up to 1855.

The earliest Parish Register entry for Islay is 1770 at Bowmore: there are large gaps in all the registers, many entries are damaged and, in some cases, there are no registers at all prior to 1830s.

---

26 KILCHOMAN PARISH was an ancient parish, named after the Celtic saint Coman who established a church in the north east of the parish. The parish was united with that of Kilarrow from 1618 to 1769, when it again acquired separate parochial status. In 1899 a new, Norman-style church was built between Port Charlotte and Bruichladdich villages. This church, St Kiarans, is now the parish church. Kilchoman was linked with Portnahaven parish in 1962, and further linked with Kilmeny in 2006.

The Isle of Jura can be found off the west coast of Scotland, a few miles north-east from the island of Islay, separated by the Sound of Islay.

In the mid 18th century as part of the 'Laird's plans for the grounds of Islay house', the entire population of the village of Kilarrow, in the parish of Kilarrow, was moved to the new-planned, coastal village of Bowmore, built to re-house those who were not directly involved in the work of the Islay Estate of the Campbells of Shawfield.

Kilarrow (Islay), by James Miller in 1772

Originally, small fields were left between the rows of houses to allow the inhabitants to grow their food for their family and keep a milking cow, but these fields now have houses built on them. A pier and harbour area was also built to enable the residents to provide for themselves by fishing. Only the churchyard of the old village of Kilarrow remains today.

John Spence (Gran Stevenson's great-great-grandfather) was born about 1767 in Kilarrow, Bowmore on the Island of Islay, Scotland. John was a farmer or more likely a crofter or agricultural labourer. Circa 1798, John married Effie Ferguson. Effie (Gran Stevenson's great-great-grandmother) was born about 1770. They had three children, all born at Bowmore, Kilarrow Parish: Barbara was born on 13 October 1799; John in1800 and Janet on 26 December 1801.

The Round Church, Bowmore, now the parish church of Kilarrow, was built in 1767 by Daniel Campbell of Shawfield and Islay. He was a wealthy Glasgow merchant, a signatory to the Act of Union between Scotland and England in 1707, and a member for the City of Glasgow in the first

The Round Church, Bowmore

United Kingdom Parliament. For a total purchase price of £12,000, he became Laird of Islay in the year 1726. The story is that the church was built in a circular shape to make sure that "there were no corners in the church in which the Devil could hide".

The separate entrance doors to Portnahaven Church

Circa 1820, Barbara Spence (Gran Stevenson's great-grandmother) and John Anderson (Gran Stevenson's great-grandfather born in 1783) were married. They had six children: Ann in 1821; Helen in 1825; Isabella in 1827; Robert in 1829; William in 1833 and Barbara in 1837. In the 1841 Census the family are recorded as staying at Cladvil (Cladaville)[27] a croft near Portnahaven.

In the 1841 census for Kilarrow, Helen, aged 16, is recorded as still being with the family in Cladavil, Portnahaven on the Island of Islay. The following is a transcription of the 1841 Census of Kildalton, Kilarrow, Portnhaven[28], Oa, Kilmeny, and Kilchomen Islay, Scotland. The family number given is to allow for searching. It was not part of the original census.

---

[27] Present day Cladville Dairy is probably not the house recorded in the 1841 Census as being occupied by the Anderson family. However, a short distance away from the present house, and dating from the late 18th or early 19th century, is the turf-covered remains of a deserted farmstead consisting of three ruined buildings and a probable corn drying kiln. A nearby, later-built, stone-walled enclosure, probably an old sheepfold, reinforces the assumption that the Anderson family was possibly evicted to be replaced by sheep.

[28] Portnahaven (Port na Abhainne) is a 19th century, planned village that lies at the south-western tip of the peninsula, the Rhinns of Islay. It was built around a small, sheltered fishing harbour, seven miles from Port Charlotte and very much the "end of the road" in this part of the island where the main employment had been crofting.

Parish	Family	Pg	Place	First Name	Surname	Sex	Age	Occupation	Where Born
Portnhaven	95	5	Cladavil	John	Anderson	Male	58		ARY
Portnhaven	95	5	Cladavil	Ann	Anderson	Female	20		ARY
Portnhaven	95	5	Cladavil	Helen	Anderson	Female	16		ARY
Portnhaven	95	5	Cladavil	Isabella	Anderson	Female	14		ARY
Portnhaven	95	5	Cladavil	Robert	Anderson	Male	12		ARY
Portnhaven	95	5	Cladavil	William	Anderson	Male	8		ARY
Portnhaven	95	5	Cladavil	Barbara	Anderson	Female	4		ARY

Barbara, the mother, is not mentioned in the 1841 census record. Initially it was assumed that she had died about 1837 in Cladvil, Portnahaven Parish when her daughter Barbara was born.

However ten years later in the 1851 census records for Islay there is no mention of the family and it is reasonable to assume that the whole family had been 'cleared' or had migrated[29] to the Lowlands

---

[29]   In the early 1800's, with its mild climate and reasonable land fertility and with the wide-spread availability of the potato and basic health care, Islay's population in the crofting and farming communities rapidly increased to about 18,000 people. Traditional crofting, however, could not the support such a huge rise in population nor, more importantly, meet the financial needs of commercially-minded landowners who were intent on establishing more profitable sheep farming that needed more land and fewer people. Landowners were now demanding increased rents in cash rather than rent in kind or in labour. They forcefully evicted tenants who were unable to pay on time and those who would not go willingly. On Islay a programme of clearances into the newly established fishing ports such as Portnahaven, Port Charlotte and Port Ellen as well as enforced emigration to the Scottish Lowlands reduced the total population of the island to about 4,000 people.

OUR ANCESTORS IN THE EAST COAST OF SCOTLAND

GRAN STEVENSON

Janet Ferguson (Gran Stevenson's great-great-great-grandmother) was born about 1745, in Newbattle Parish[30], Midlothian, Scotland.

James Porteous (Gran Stevenson's great-great-great-grandfather) was born about 1745. Aged about 24, James Porteous married Janet Ferguson, also aged about 24, on 21st July 1769 in Liberton Parish[31], Midlothian, Scotland.

Their daughter, Margaret, (Gran Stevenson's great-great-grandmother) was born in 1770. On 28th June 1789 in Stenton, Dunbar Margaret, aged 19, married David Smith, aged about 28. He was born about 1760 in East Lothian, Scotland. Richard, their son, was born in 1796.

---

[30] *"NEWBATTLE, (or Newbotle) is a parish in the county of Edinburgh, Scotland. It comprises the village of its own name, also the villages of Stobhill, Easthouses, and Newton Grange. A large portion of the land is generally rich and fertile,, except in the upper district, where the soil is marshy and muiry upon a cold till. It is abundant in orchards and gardens. The district is also productive of good coal, lime, and sandstone.*
(Description from The National Gazetteer (1868)

[31] *"LIBERTON, is a parish in the county of Edinburgh, Scotland, 2 miles South of Edinburgh. It contains the villages of Upper (or Over) Liberton, Liberton Kirk, and Nether Liberton, with Gilmerton and Green End. The parish, which lies at the base of the Pentland hills, is exceedingly populous, and its coal mines and lime works are most extensive and valuable. There are several sandstone quarries in the neighbourhood.*
Description from The National Gazetteer (1868)

Andrew Knox (Gran Stevenson's great-great-great-grandfather) was a Sawyer in Leith, Scotland. About 1770 he married Grizell Singer (Gran Stevenson's great-great-great-grandmother). Their daughter, Janet, was born on 27th June 1771. Janet married James McLachlan, born about 1760. Their daughter, Janet (Gran Stevenson's great-great-grandmother) was born about 1796.

Richard Smith (Gran Stevenson's great-grandfather), born on 29 July 1796, in Stenton[32], Dunbar, East Lothian, Scotland, to David Smith and Margaret Smith [Porteous] married Janet McLachlan(Gran Stevenson's great-grandmother), born about 1796 to James McLachlan and Janet McLachlan [Knox].

The marriage took place on 15th December 1822 in Old Monklands Parish, Coatbridge, Scotland. They had five children, James was born in 1827, Janet was born in 1830, Richard in 1832, Margaret was born in 1835 and Agnes Smith in 1839

In 1851, aged about 54, Richard was a Grocer and Spirit Dealer in Langloan, Old Monklands Parish. He died on 27 June 1860, aged 63, in Langloan, Old Monklands[33] Parish and was buried in June 1860 in Old Monklands Church Yard. Janet died (old age) on 18 April 1879, aged about 82, in Smith's Land, Langloan[34], Old Monklands Parish.

---

[32]   *Stenton is a parish and village in East Lothian, Scotland. It is bounded on the north by parts of the parishes of Prestonkirk and Dunbar, on the east by Spott and on the west by Whittingehame. The name is said to be of Saxon derivation.*
From: A Topographical Dictionary of Scotland (1846).

[33]   A description of Coatbridge (Old Monklands Parish) is given in a book on the industries of Scotland by Bremner in 1869.
"Though *Coatbridge is a most interesting seat of industry, it is anything but beautiful. Dense clouds of smoke roll over it incessantly, and a coat of black dust overlies everything. To appreciate Coatbridge, it must be visited at night, when it presents a most extraordinary and startling spectacle. From the steeple of the parish church, which stands on a considerable eminence, the flames of no fewer than fifty blast furnaces may be seen*".

[34]   *"LANGLOAN, a village, in the parish of Old Monkland, Middle ward of the county of Lanark, is one of the principal villages of the many in this great mining and manufacturing parish: it is situated on the road from Airdrie to Glasgow, and has of late years increased exceedingly in extent and population"*.

THE JOINING OF THE FAMILIES FROM
THE ISLANDS AND THE EAST COAST

The census of 30th March, 1851 records the Anderson family as living at 103, Langloan, Old Monklands and the father, John Anderson, as a Spirit Merchant[35].

Some of the Anderson family appear to have returned to Islay because they are recorded in the 1861 Census for Portnahaven, Islay. Barbara, the mother is recorded as head of the family, a widow. (John, the father, died in the years between the 1851 and 1861 census taking). She is also recorded as a Spirit Merchant and the family live in the public house in Portnahaven. Her death certificate dated 15th June 1862 records her as the Innkeeper[36].

On 14th October 1851 in Old Monklands Parish Lanark, James Smith, an Iron Agent, (Gran Stevenson's grandfather who was born on 29th July 1827 to Richard Smith and Janet Smith [McLachlan]) married Helen Anderson (Gran Stevenson's' grandmother who was born on 10th February 1825, in Cladaville, Kilchoman Parish, Island of Islay, to John Anderson and his wife Barbara Anderson [Spence])

---

[35] Whisky distilling started on farms all over Scotland and, especially on the west coast, islands. Farming had always been tough on the islands because of a lack of good quality farming land and whisky distilling was regarded as just another farm product. Whisky was believed by many to have medicinal qualities that maintained health, prolonged life and cured colic, palsy, smallpox and a host of other ailments. Simple stills came to be found in most rural homesteads and homemade whisky became an essential part of daily living and for paying the rent.

[36] The present day, quaint little pub down at the harbour looks like a private house. In Gaelic it is called 'An Tigh Seinnse', which means 'the house of singing'.

James was an Iron Merchant's Clerk. He died on 21st December 1890, aged 63, in Denniston Parish, Lanark. Helen died on 23rd May 1900, aged 75. Janet, born in 1853, was the eldest of the eight children born to them.

Janet Smith and James Millar married on the 8th November 1872, at 77, Glebe Street, Glasgow. Their fifth child, a daughter Agnes Smith Millar (Gran Stevenson), was born, on 30th November 1881, at 11 Mossvale Street, Paisley.

The 1901 Census records Agnes Millar (Gran Stevenson), her father and mother and her eight brothers and sisters as living at 35, McKerrell Street, Paisley. McKerrell Street was regarded as being a middle-class, residential area of the town.

Her father, James Millar aged 54, was a Blacksmith[37] but, by that date, had retired. Her brother John Henry, aged 26, was a Gas Meter Inspector. Her sister Marion, aged 24 was a Thread Winder, James, aged 22, was an Engineer's Patternmaker. Agnes, aged 19, was a Domestic Servant[38].

David, aged 16, was a Brickwork Labourer He emigrated to Canada where, in 1913, he married Agnes Wilson. They had two children. Her sister Janet,

---

[37]   Blacksmiths, working in extremely hot, poorly-lit, dirty buildings, had a far higher economic and social position than farm or factory workers. The work of the village blacksmith was vital to life in both town and country. He could shoe horses and make and mend tools and farming equipment. He also made more common objects such as door hinges, locks, bolts, pots, pans and nails.
       However, in the Victorian Era, semi-skilled labour using machinery in newly built factories were able to turn out, faster and more cheaply, tools and products that were once handmade by blacksmiths. During this time many out-of-work blacksmiths entered the new heavy industries making railway axles and wheels and other parts for trains. They also worked in ship-building and in the engineering and textile industries, building and repairing machines.

[38]   In the Victorian era, according to the census records of 1851, 1861 and 1871, domestic service was a major employer in Britain. With few labour-saving appliances, everything was done by hand. A large house required a large staff to clear the ashes, lay the fire in the grate, clean the rooms, make the beds, cook and do the laundry.
       Even the more modest middle class households of shopkeepers, innkeepers and small traders would have had one or two servants, usually a maid-of-all-work and a cook, whose duties were regarded essential to a well-run household.

aged 14, was a Silk Finisher, her brother William, aged 13, was a Railway Clerk. Her brother, Hugh, aged 9 and her sister, Barbara, aged 5, were scholars. Hugh died in Florida, USA. In 1915, Barbara married Howard Hill Manzie in Scotland.

Though Barbara and Howard emigrated to Ontario, Canada, Barbara returned regularly to Paisley to visit her relatives. On one of her visits she donated, to the Paisley Museum, her mother's Paisley pattern Wedding Shawl.[39]

In the 1901 census her sister Helen Anderson Millar, aged 25, is not recorded with the rest of the family. In 1898 she had married James Murray, aged 24, in 17, Mossvale Street, Paisley.

Paisley High Church

Gran Stevenson's father (James Millar) died, aged 58, in 1906. Her paternal grandparents were John Millar, a Wood Sawyer, and Henrietta Wilson who were married on 27 July, 1834 in Paisley High Church, Oakshaw Brae, Paisley. The old parish marriage record shows that John came from the Paisley High Church parish and that Henrietta came from the parish of Neilston, a village near to the town of Barrhead and a few miles from Paisley.

Gran Stevenson's mother (Janet Millar (born Smith)) died, aged 66, in 1919. Her mother's sister, Barbara Joan Smith married James McIntyre in

---

[39]  In the 19th century, expensive, hand-woven Kashmiri shawls were an essential part of a 'well-dressed' woman's voluminous costume. The shawl, an oversized square in shape draped over the shoulders, was more practical than a cloak because it could also be used as a hood in inclement weather. Reproduction Kashmiri shawls were woven on mechanical looms in Scotland, particularly in the town of Paisley, which gave its name to the design that was re-interpreted from the original Indian motif to conform to European taste. Though these shawls were less expensive than hand-woven examples it still took a full two weeks to weave the beautiful, tear-shaped paisley cone design of each shawl.

1875 and migrated to Australia. Her mother's brother, James Anderson Smith married Mary Turner Seaton in 1897 and emigrated to Canada.

Since so many of Gran Stevenson's brothers, sisters, uncles and aunts had emigrated in the early 1900's it is not so surprising that there was little contact with that side of the family.

Our Ancestors in the West of Scotland

GRANDPA STEVENSON

George Steel (or Steil) (our great-great-great-grandfather) was born on 3 August 1788, in Abbey Parish[40], Paisley, to James Steel (or Steil) and Janet Steel (or Steil). George, aged 16, married Margaret Taylor on 25 August 1804 in Quarrelton, Abbey Parish, Paisley. They had two children, a son George in 1807 and a daughter Margaret in 1819. George was a Coal Miner.

Margaret Steel (our great-great-grandmother) was born on 12 April 1819, in Quarrelton[41] Abbey Parish, Paisley, Scotland, to George Steel and Margaret Steel [Taylor]. Margaret aged 33 married Robert Stevenson aged about 29, on 22 October 1852 in Johnstone. A son, George Steel Stevenson was born to them in 1855.

---

[40] *Situated in North East Renfrewshire the parish of Abbey, sometimes called Abbey Paisley, includes part of the town of Paisley whilst completely surrounding the Paisley burgh parishes. It also contains the town of Johnstone, the Dovecothall portion of Barrhead, and the villages of Elderslie, Thorn, Quarrelton, Inkerman, Hurlet, and Nitshill. It is surrounded by the following parishes, Renfrew, Govan in Lanarkshire, Eastwood, Neilston, Lochwinnoch and Kilbarchan.*

[41] *Quarrelton, with Johnston may be considered as a thriving town rather tthan as a village, in the west. The population consists almost entirely of colliers and miners who are employed in the extensive works in their neighbourhood. The village is very pleasantly situated, on the north side of the great road from Glasgow to Beith and it presents from morning to night, a very busy and animated scene, from the great number of travellers daily passing. This village is well supplied with excellent water.* From The new statistical account of Scotland, volume 14

Robert Stevenson (our great-great-grandfather) was born about 1823, in Linwood, Scotland. In October 1852, aged about 29, he was a Flax Mill Labourer and latterly a Gatekeeper in Johnstone. His wife, Margaret, died on 4 March 1871, aged 51, in 5, Houston Square, Johnstone.

George Steel Stevenson (our great-grandfather) was born on 5 February 1855, in Bridge of Weir, Scotland, to Robert Stevenson and Margaret Stevenson [Steel]. He was employed as a Flax Dresser.

Isabella Ramsay (our great-grandmother) was born in 1857, in Ireland, to John Ramsay and Mary Ramsay [Laverty] On 30 March 1876 aged 21, George married Isabella Ramsay, aged about 18, and employed as a Carpet Factory Worker in 5, Houston Square, Johnstone.

They had seven children, Robert Stevenson, born in 1876, Maggie (Margaret) born in 1879, George Steel in 1881, George in 1885, Annie (Ann) in 1888, Sarah in 1890 and Catherine Findlay in 1893.

When Isabella died on 14 June 1899, aged about 41, in 3 Ludovic Square, Johnstone, George married Nellie (Ellen) Kelly. George died on 21 March 1907, aged 52, in 15 High Street, Johnstone.

Gran and Grandpa Stevenson
Isa and Jessie

Robert Stevenson (Grandpa Stevenson) was born on 25 September 1876, in 5 Houston Square, Johnstone, to George Steel Stevenson and Isabella Stevenson [Ramsay]. Robert was an Engineer's Machinist. On 6 June 1902 in 35 McKerrell Street, Paisley, Agnes Smith Millar (my maternal Grandmother), aged 20, married Robert Stevenson (my maternal Grandfather), aged 25. They had two daughters, Janet Smith Stevenson born in 1903 and Isabella Ramsay Stevenson born in 1907. In the 1911 census, the family is recorded as staying at 11, Andrews Street,

Paisley and Robert's (Grandpa Stevenson's) employment as an iron driller, General Engineering.

In the Valuation Roll of 1915, Robert Stevenson[42] (Grandpa Stevenson), boilermaker, is recorded as being a tenant at 19, Underwood Lane at a rent of £10 per year (3/9d per week). (Valuation Rolls list individuals who paid over £4 yearly in rent for a property they owned or rented.) On the ground floor of number 19 there was a dairy shop and a pend[43] that led through to a farm house and stables. The tenements had been built on what had been the land belonging to the farm.

Robert Stevenson died on 6th. August 1943, aged 66, in 28 Underwood Lane, Paisley. He was buried on 9th, August 1943 in Abbey Cemetery, Thorn, Johnstone. Agnes (Smith Millar) Stevenson died on 16th, September 1957, aged 75, in 29 Crawfurd Drive, Paisley, Scotland.

Isabella Ramsey Stevenson (my mother), was born in 1907, in Paisley, Scotland, to Robert Stevenson (my maternal Grandfather) and Agnes Smith Stevenson [Millar] (my maternal Grandmother). Isabella died in 1999, aged about 92, in Johnstone, Scotland.

Allan McAlpine Vandal (my father) was born on 22nd August 1909, in 3 New Sneddon, Paisley, Scotland, to George (Jørgen) Carl Larsen Vandal (my paternal Grandfather), and Isabella Vandal [McConnachie] (my paternal Grandmother).

Allan was a butcher by trade but during the depression years of the 1930s and throughout World War 2 he sailed on the River Clyde and round

---

[42] The number of people with the name Robert Stevenson makes it difficult when accessing records. The information from the 1911 census is correct because the whole family is recorded but the valuation record for 1920 is assumed because only Robert Stevenson is recorded though the employment is similar. When the census for 1921 becomes available it should confirm the accuracy of the assumption.

[43]  A Pend is a covered passageway that passes through a building, from a street through to a courtyard. It has rooms directly above it and is designed for vehicular rather than exclusively pedestrian access.

the Western Islands of Scotland as mate on board the Clyde Puffer s.s. Stormlight owned by Ross and Marshall, Ltd., ship-owners, stevedores, coal merchants and managers of the Light shipping company, Greenock, Renfrewshire, Scotland.

In 1948 he came ashore and returned to his trade as butcher. Allan died in 1981, aged about 71, in Paisley, Renfrewshire, Scotland. He was cremated in 1981 in Woodside Crematorium, Paisley, Renfrewshire, Scotland.

Since the 1915 Valuation Roll records that both the Vandal family and the Stevenson family lived in Underwood Lane it is reasonable to assume that Allan and Isabella knew each other as children. I also remember seeing a photograph of my father as a young lad, standing next to a pony and cart. I was told that he helped the local dairyman deliver milk.

Carl, Robert, Allan, Allan and Isa Vandal

Isabella aged about 24 married Allan McAlpine Vandal aged 22 on 16th, December, 1931 in the High Church, Paisley.

They had four children, Carl, Agnes, Robert and Allan.

Carl George Vandal was born on 23rd, September 1932, in Barshaw Maternity Hospital, Paisley, Scotland.

On 13th, September 1969 in the Scots Presbyterian Church, Clayfield, Brisbane, Australia, Carl George Vandal, aged 36, married Cathie aged 24. Cathie (Catherine Anne) Vandal [Edwards] was born on 31st, July 1945, in Australia, to William Harold Edwards and Frances Muriel Edwards [Fletcher]. They had two children, Katrina and Christian.

Katrina Frances Vandal born on 31st, May 1971, in Brisbane, Australia, married Steven Gorton in Brisbane, Australia. They had two children: Jessica Anne Gorton in 1991 and Dylan James Gorton in 1992. They were divorced. Isla Maree Gorton was born 6th November, 2013 to Jessica Anne Gorton and her partner Kyle Morris.

Christian Allan Vandal born on 4th, July 1974, in Brisbane, Australia, married Rae-Maree Barry (Mannion) aged about 41, on 18th, November 2006 in Brisbane, Australia. Rae-Maree's first husband was Derek Barry.

Agnes Millar Vandal was born on 19th, January 1937, in Barshaw Maternity Hospital, Paisley, Scotland. She died, of measles and Bronchial Pneumonia, on 28th, March 1938, aged about 1, in Paisley, Scotland.

Robert Stevenson Vandal was born on 2nd, November 1939, in Barshaw Maternity Hospital, Paisley, Scotland.

On 16th, December 1966 in het Leger des Heils, Prinsegracht, s'Gravenhage, Nederland, Robert, Stevenson Vandal, aged 27, married Trudie (Geertuida C.E.) Vandal [van Zaalen], born on 3rd, May 1940, in Den Haag, Nederland, to Frans P. van Zaalen and Adrienne C. van Zaalen [Leeuwarden]. Trudie died on 5th, April 2007, aged 66, in Ayrshire Hospice, Ayr, Scotland.

They had two sons, Carl, Stuart and adopted Jeanne.

Carl Terence Alexander Vandal was born on 29th, April 1969, in Edinburgh, Scotland. Carl was dedicated (christened) on 28th, September 1969 in het Leger des Heils, Prinsegracht 57, s'Gravenhage, Nederland by Commissioner Westergaard.

Between August 1974 and June 1980, from the age of about 5, he attended Loanhead Primary School, Kilmarnock, Ayrshire, Scotland. Between August 1980 and June 1985, from the age of about 11, he attended Kilmarnock Academy, Kilmarnock, Ayrshire, Scotland.

Between August 1985 and June 1986, from the age of about 16, he attended Marr College, Troon, Ayrshire, Scotland (Secondary).

Between September 1986 and May 1990, from the age of about 17, Carl attended Strathclyde University, Glasgow, Scotland where he obtained a BA degree in Pure Maths.

On 31st, May 2002 in Coombe Abbey, Coventry, England, Carl, aged 33, married Katy Halford, born on 30th, July 1980 to Philip Halford and Rosalyn Halford [George]. They had two daughters: Rhiannon Faye Vandal in 2005 and Freya Vandal in 2006

Stuart Bertram Alisdair Vandal was born on 25th, November 1970, in Dundee, Scotland. He was dedicated (christened) in 1971, in The Salvation Army, Brechin, Scotland by Colonel Emerson.

Between August 1975 and June 1982, from the age of about 4, he was educated in Loanhead Primary School, Kilmarnock, Ayrshire, Scotland (Primary). Between August 1982 and June 1987, from the age of about 11, he attended Kilmarnock Academy, Kilmarnock, Ayrshire, Scotland (Secondary). Between September 1987 and May 1991, from the age of about 16, he attended Strathclyde University, Glasgow, Scotland where he obtained a BA (hons) degree in Pure Maths.

Jeanne Lauren Gass [Batty] was born on 30th, November 1960, in Liverpool, England. She was adopted by Robert Stevenson Vandal and Trudie (Geertruida C.E.) Vandal [van Zaalen].

Jeanne, aged 22, married George Gass on 19th, February 1983 in Henderson Church, Kilmarnock, Scotland. They had two children, Ari Gass in 1988 and Daena Gass in 1990. They were divorced

Allan Vandal was born on 13th, May 1942, in 9, Auchentorlie Quadrant, Paisley, Renfrewshire, Scotland. In 1957, aged about 15, he left school, The John Neilson Institution, Paisley.

Between 1957 and 1962, from the age of about 15, he was an apprentice marine engineer in Paisley, Renfrewshire, Scotland. Between 9th September 1963 and 6th January 1964, from the age of about 21, he was a Marine engineer in the Merchant Navy on board the motor vessel "Escelante",

Royal Mail Lines Shipping Company. Allan only spent a few months on the "Escelante[44]", because he felt unhappy with the ship and the owners.

Between 1975 and 4th February 1987, from the age of about 33, he was a Maintenance Engineer on Morecambe Central Pier[45].

Aged 25, Allan married Sue (Susan Marjorie) Vandal [Hale] on 23rd, June 1967 in the Register Office Bath, Somerset, England. They divorced on 11th, November 1983, when Allan was aged 41, in Lancaster County Court, England.

Between 18th May 1987 and 1999, from the age of about 45, Allan was an Amusement Rides Manager in Flamingo Land Theme Park, Kirby Misperton, Malton, North Yorkshire, England.

On 20th June 2000 in St. Catherine's Hospice, Scarborough, England, Allan, aged 58 years, died of cancer of the palate. He was buried overlooking Flamingo Land Theme Park in the cemetery of Kirby Misperton Parish Church, Malton, North Yorkshire, England.

Carl Vandal, Australia, 11th April 2002

FAMILY HISTORY

I have a fairly good recollection of stories I have heard since childhood, and while there is no doubt that to a greater or lesser extent these could be factual, without some substantiation, the best they will do is to point your enquiries into a number of different directions, some of which might yield the answers you need.

---

[44]   M. V. *Escalante* was built in 1955 by Harland & Wolff Ltd, Govan for Royal Mail Lines Ltd. In 1965 the Royal Mail Line was acquired by Furness, Withy & Company Ltd, which in turn was later bought by C Y Tung (Hong Kong) then Hamburg-Süd (DE). In 1970 she was sold to Panama and renamed *Manes P.* On her first trip for her new owners on 02/02/1970 she grounded on the rock breakwater at St Johns, New Brunswick and was lost.

[45]   Morecambe Central Pier opened on 25th March 1869 and closed at Easter 1986 after decking collapsed at the seaward end. A fire on 4th February 1987 damaged the amusement arcade at the shoreward end. A Council report condemned the pier and demolition began in March 1992.

GRANNY VANDAL: She was certainly 'one of a kind: I only remember her in her later years when she was permanently 'bedridden', she ruled the roost from her bed which had been moved into the living—room at Gallowhill, and she treated Aunt Isa abominably, as a combination cook, housemaid, nursemaid and general dogs— body. One of her favourite sayings was, 'Isa made a pot of Soup/ Stew/ Mince/ (or whatever), and it's no fit for pigs to eat! - do you want some???'

Granny's maiden name was McConnachie, and she had some connection with the Fleming family of Greenock. (Fleming and Reid Woollen Mills, and wool shops). I don't know if Fleming was her mother's maiden name, but it is a possibility. One of the Flemings, one of granny's cousins, was somehow connected to Charles de Gaulle, either his mother, or related to his mother. I know that Granny referred to de Gaulle as a cousin, but I don't know the exact relationship.

Granny was a widow when she married Grandpa, and her previous married name could have been Watt. I remember visiting a very old lady in Greenock with our cousin Chas. Flood and he called her Granny Watt, and introduced me to her, and she then referred to me as 'Allan's wee boy'.. but since I was about 23 at the time, and Granny Vandal died when I was about 10 I can't imagine that she was Granny's mother-in-law, but she must have had some co-lateral relationship.

Both Chas. and I had attended the Watt College, (he doing R/T before going into the navy during the war, and me, before going to sea after leaving school) and I remember some comment being made over the co— incidence, since the Watt connection was the same family line as Jas. Watt after whom the college was named.

The story has it that Aunt Lizzy (Flood) lived with a Granny Watt during a time when Granny Vandal sailed with Grandpa. I believe Granny was a Catholic when she and Grandpa got married, and this caused a family rift- with her family. A result of this was that Aunt Lizzie was brought-up a catholic - and Aunt Mary was brought up protestant- I'm not sure, but this suggests that Mary and Lizzie were from the first marriage.

Charley Flood would possibly be in his late eighties or early nineties by now, but if it was possible to get in touch with him, he might have better information on this side of the family. Chas. got married around 1962/3, to a Bunty O'Neill. (I don't know Bunty's given name).

Chas and Bunty were engaged for years but because he was a freelance writer, (and always broke) they didn't get around to getting married until quite late. Bunty's brother had a betting shop in Port Glasgow, and as far as I know, Chas got a job with him as an accountant. If Chas or Bunty are still alive, and you can trace them, this might give you some information on this connection. As far as I know, they moved into a council-house at the top of the hill on the Kilmalcom Road, (Lisle Hill?), Port Glasgow.

Aunt Lizzie and Uncle Jack attended the church at the town end of Cartsdike Road. - Auntie Lizzie was one of those very devout parishioners who would go to early mass each morning then go home and make the breakfast. There might be some leads to Chas and Bunty in the parish records. A boy I knew who lived in Henderson Street (off Underwood Lane) went to Italy (via Ireland) during the war to study for the priesthood, and at a later time he was the priest in Aunt Lizzie's church, his name was Andrew Cunningham. His mother and Gran Stevenson were friends. Andrew knew Aunt Lizzie well, and if he's alive, he'll be retired, being in his mid-seventies, but a possible lead to the Floods.

When Granny's first husband died, she was left with a big house, and the necessity to generate an income. The house was in Rue End Street just on the bend where West India Dock becomes Rue-End. I used to pass it every day going to and from college.

At that time it was a suite of consulting rooms for a group of doctors. It was still there when we were on holiday in 1997, and it was still consulting rooms. I pointed it out to Cathy at the time. Apart front its size, it was black with grime, and I don't think Cathy was too impressed.

As far as I know, Granny opened the house as an 'Up-Market boarding house, catering to ship's officers, commercial travellers, etc. I don't know if she managed to make it pay because she apparently kept on her staff and was well known to be a soft-touch for any one with a hard-luck story.

When she married Grandpa, I believe he was also quite comfortably off so she left the house to be run by someone else so that she could sail with Grandpa for a couple of years.

I don't know what happened at that point, but she either sold or relinquished the house to the staff and tenants. It is possible that if there was some form of dispute with her former in-laws she might just have given the house over. That would be in keeping with her eccentricity.

I've heard the story about the hats, but there were other bizarre things she would do. During the war when food was very scarce, Granny took a 'Notion' to have some tripe. Offal as such wasn't rationed, but it was hard to come by. Granny asked our mother to get her some because Aunt Isa had tried without luck, (And was therefore "useless"). So trailing me, and with you in the pram, we trekked down to Beaton's abattoir at the corner of Caledonia St and Greenock Road looking for tripe. Dad knew the Beatons from when he was serving his time as a butcher, and Dan Beaton was in my class at school, so after introductions and namedropping we trekked back to Gallowhill with this parcel of tripe. When Granny saw it she wasn't too happy, because it hadn't been cleaned but was as it came out of the cow. Well there was a blow-up and Granny was lucky not to end up wearing a couple of hanks of cow's innards as a scarf. We didn't visit Gallowhill for a couple of weeks until we got a postcard from Granny wanting to know if 'the weans were sick?'

Being an invalid for many years, and very ill towards the end, when she took 'notions' everyone did what they could to get what she wanted. At one stage she took a notion for some ham, not just any ham which was almost impossible to get, but Belfast Ham.

Aunt Isa went to the shop where they were 'registered'[46] and managed to get a couple of ounces of quite inferior fatty ham. Granny blew-up, and Mum asked Dad for a loan of his Merchant-Navy ration book. (self-messing

---

[46]   During World War 2 food was rationed. Each person in a family had a 'ration book' and had to register as a customer at a butcher's shop and could only purchase a limited quantity of meat from that shop.

crews[47] had a fairly generous victualling allowance, and their ration cards could be used anywhere.). So off we went by tramcar to Glasgow. There was a Belfast Ham and Butter shop in the Cowcaddens, and we were able to get the ham, properly wrapped in the shop-branded paper, and Granny was happy. It wouldn't have mattered if it was the same ham as Aunt Isa had got, as long as it was wrapped in the right paper.

Granny was very friendly with a Greenock family called Crawford and at one time she lent them money to open a Tearoom/Restaurant in East Hamilton St. just about opposite the driveway to Greenock Central railway station. When I was in college it was still running, and every one in Greenock knew 'Miss Crawford's'. Dad told me that if I let them know who I was, I wouldn't have to pay the bill. Don't know, didn't try it!! It was a funny set-up; Downstairs at street level, it had plain wooden tables, and workers in their overalls would be in there eating. Up-stairs was very posh. Suits, ties, and quite a bit dearer. I suppose that was to pay for the table-cloths and napkins, etc. I don't know if the Crawfords ever paid her back, the suggestion was that Granny could have sold them up to get what she was owed, but she never did.

As you can see, Granny wasn't much of a financial manager. She hadn't been brought up to it, and as a result money didn't have much value to her until they didn't have any. I don't know much about their other properties. I know they had a cottage at Kyle of Lochalsh, because during the school holidays Dad and one of his friends would make their pocket money pushing cars up the planks on to the ferry, particularly 3 wheelers which needed an extra plank.

GRANDPA: I know that Grandpa was born on Bornholm, and I was told that he ran away to sea after some family dispute. What the town was I don't know. He apparently never got in touch with family afterwards. I can remember him telling me that when he was sailing in that part of the Baltic, he could sometimes see his family's house from the deck, because it was the only one in their town/village, which had a red roof.

I understand that Uncle George went to Denmark sometime after the 1st World War, and visited some cousins that he managed to get in touch with,

---

47   During World War 2 Clyde puffer crews were officially in the Merchant Navy and had to buy their own food and were therefore allowed to do so whatever port they might be in.

but any contacts he had with them would have ended with the German occupation during the 2nd World War and I didn't hear much about it.

Grandpa retired early in life, but at one time he owned a sailing boat. Dad called it a schooner and it traded up and down the west coast. Thinking about it and the type of coastal trade it probably did, I think it could have been a 'Gabbard' as far as I know, they were lugger rigged, and probably a bit like the Thames barges that used to run- up and down- the channel coast, a bit like a Dutch 'schut' in some ways.

He eventually had a couple of Puffers. (including the 'X'). During the depression, he came out of retirement and ran one of them, and laid up the others (possibly two). He crewed the one he ran- by rotating between George, Sammy, James, Jack Flood and Allan MacAlpine, so that they could have a chance of a wage, interspersed with periods on the dole. He went broke, and he sold out to Sam Warnock and Ross § Marshall. I don't know what went where, but I believe the 'X' was arrested for an unpaid fuel bill, and with the sheriff's warrant tying her up she eventually owed more in harbour dues than she was worth... and there she lay.

Sammy had a big family, but you probably know all about them from Carl's correspondent. Uncle James had two children, Iris and Jim. Iris is probably about 61 or thereabouts, and Jim is a couple of years younger,

The only member of the family you might not know about is Uncle Bobby. He was killed at the battle of Arras, in 1917. He was in one of the high numbered battalions of the Argylls. Cathy and I saw his name in the Honour Roll of the regiment in the war Memorial in Edinburgh castle. Uncle George was in the same unit when Bobby was killed.

Well Robert, I don't know if anything in this adds to your family knowledge, as you can see it is mostly apocryphal, but you might manage to get some pointers as to where to enquire next.

Yours Aye

Carl and Cathy

THE TENEMENT HOUSE

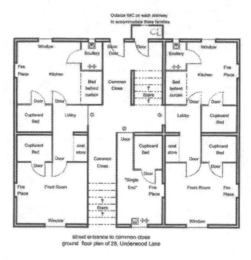

From the mid 1800's to early 1900's, tenements were designed and built to house the influx of migrants who flooded in to the industrial towns from the Highlands and Islands of Scotland as well as the thousands of Irish who were escaping the potato famine in Ireland.

Since the basic design of the accommodation could be adapted easily to suit the incomes of the different social classes of the work-force needed for the industrial expansion of foundries, mills, mines and shipyards, the tenement building became a distinctive feature of traditional Glasgow architecture that extended into the neighbouring towns including Paisley.

These tenements were usually built side by side to form a continuous street frontage of three or four-storey high blocks of flats.

Tenement flats, built for the "working-class" and their families, had poor facilities. Each floor housed three families in very basic one-roomed ("single-end") and two-roomed ("room and kitchen") apartments accessed from landings off a common stairway. The "room and kitchen" consisted of one room, usually kept and used only for special occasions, and a slightly larger room that the family occupied as a combined kitchen, dining room, living room and "bedroom" all in one. A black, cast-iron, kitchen range, heated by the fire, would take up most of one wall. The coal was kept in a bunker in the little lobby inside the front door. By the early 1900's there would be a sink, with a cold water tap, and a gas cooker in the scullery and the 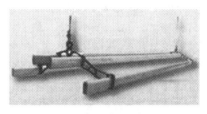 gas lighting was often replaced by electricity. Washing would be hung in the kitchen on the clothes pulley overhead in the kitchen.

There were no internal bathrooms or water closets. To take a bath, water had to be heated on the kitchen range to fill a tin bath in front of the fire. In such conditions personal privacy was difficult and personal private space was just not available. Despite this families normally had a fierce personal pride and aspired to improving themselves and their circumstances

With less than ten square metres of overcrowded floor space, recessed beds, known as "box-beds" or "hole-in-the-wall beds", were a common feature. The kitchen usually had a bed closet, enclosed within a cupboard, and a curtained alcove containing a "set in" bed raised high off the floor to provide useful storage space underneath. The long curtains could be closed for privacy or to hide the bed during the day. The space below the bed was normally used for storage, often for another folding bed which could be pulled out at night time.

The one room home, or 'single end' was small with a floor space of approximately 14 feet by 11.5 feet. The number of people per one room home varied from place to place, and street to street but in the early years of the 1900's the average number was five. Depending on a family's individual circumstances, many tenants would take in lodgers to help pay the rent.

The tenants of each close had to share a toilet with their neighbours. This was originally a "privy round the back", an outside soil closet in the back-court. Also situated in the back-court were the communal middens (dust/garbage/trash bins), the shared wash-houses and the drying areas.

For their weekly laundry, the resident families within a close were each allocated a different day the week and a time to use the wash-house, where there was a tub that could be heated by a coal fire. Families had to supply their own coal, wringer and drying line. Each family also shared, in a rota system, the task of keeping clean the communal areas of the close, stairs, landings and toilets.

The Act of 1892 was intended to force tenement landlords to provide at least indoor toilet facilities for all their tenants. However, to comply with the legislation, landlords had brick stack constructions housing communal, "indoor" W.C.s (water closets) quickly and cheaply added to the rear of already existing buildings. These were accessed from the stair landings of the tenement by the three families on that landing.

Typical back court of tenement blocks

The communal close entrance to the tenement would usually signify the quality of the building and the residents. Most "working class" closes had no entrance door and the plasterwork walls were painted and stencilled or just whitewashed. They would have pipe-clayed edges to the stone steps.

In a number of cases, tenements built to very high standards had the external appearance of the more luxurious terraced houses. The "better class" close entrance had doors (sometimes with locks) and expensive patterned tiles covering the walls of the close and the entire stairways to the top landing of the building. Tenements flats, with a bedroom, a parlour, a kitchen and bathroom, were built for the "better-off".

For even wealthier people, there were larger flats, built to very high standards with four, five or even more rooms. However, even well-off tenement dwellers usually paid rent to a landlord for their homes rather than own them.

ADDITIONAL INFORMATION ON GRANNY VANDAL'S MATERNAL ANCESTORS

Thomas Cashore, my great-great grandfather, was born circa 1813 in Wexford Co. Wexford, Ireland to William Cashore, my great-great-great grandfather a soldier, and his wife Isabella McMillan.

In the early 1800's the British Government[48] sited Richmond barracks at Templemore. The barracks, one of the largest in Ireland, consisted of 2 squares, surrounded by company lines, stores, married quarters, officer's mess, military prison, church and hospital. Completely surrounded by a high wall, with protective/defensive posts at each corner, it had accommodation for 25 officers, married quarters for 48 other ranks, and 767 unmarried personnel. A total of 36 hospital beds and 15 guardroom

---

[48] Up until the late 1700's, the tasks of maintaining the peace, countering increasing insurgent activities in Ireland and defending the kingdom from invasion was successfully achieved by the small number of British regular regiments. The war with Revolutionary France from 1793 increased the demand for troops and significantly altered the dynamics of the British army in Ireland.

The shortage of troops required to fight in campaigns in the Caribbean and on the Continent led to a rapid reduction in the number of regular infantrymen in Ireland and Britain augmented its military forces by raising 38 Irish militia regiments.

In the meantime, since only a few regiments of the newly established Irish militia were operational and the Irish recruited regular regiments were being immediately shipped out of the kingdom once they had reached full strength, an immediate solution was found in the posting of English and Scottish fencibles to Ireland. A system of annual rotation was introduced which saw most Irish militia battalions serving at various locations throughout the kingdom.

cells were located within the complex as well as stabling for 27 officer's horses.

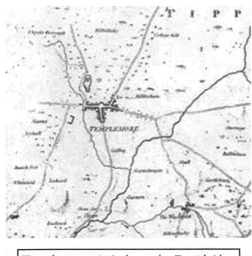

Templemore 1814. drawn by David Aher

Between construction in 1809 and Irish Independence in 1922, almost 100 different Regiments of the British Army served in Templemore. These included the 11th Depot Battalion, 59th Glasgow Regiment, Tipperary Artillery Regiment, 4th Battalion, Dublin Fusilier, Munster Fusiliers and the Northamptonshire Regiment. During the War of Independence (Ireland), the Northamptonshire Regiment was based at the Barracks and conducted reprisals in the town.

Along with the economic benefits which accrued to a town as a result of having a barracks in the locality, The British army was also a critical source of employment for Irishmen, and huge numbers enlisted, for a variety of reasons.

Granny Vandal's Maternal Ancestors and the Potato Famine in Ireland

Thomas Cashore, my great-great grandfather, was a shoemaker to trade. His children were born in Co Donegal. Isabella, my great grandmother, was born in 1837, his eldest son, William was born in 1840, Elizabeth in 1843, Sarah in 1845, James in 1846 and Jane who was born in 1848. His wife, Jane died in 1850. After her death I believe they left Ireland possibly because of the famine, the starvation, famine-related diseases, and scenes of unimaginable mass suffering they had witnessed and endured.

In 1845 a third of the potato crop in Ireland was destroyed by blight, which quickly spread, causing the crop to fail entirely in 1846 and although there was little blight in 1847 too few potatoes had been planted for the harvest to be of any use. Crops failed again in 1848. Only a single crop, the potato, failed. No other crops were affected.

A significant proportion of the Irish population lived close to total poverty and was heavily dependent on potatoes and buttermilk. The amount of potatoes consumed by labourers was reckoned to be at least eight pounds of potatoes per day when they formed the sole diet, the wife ate six pounds and the children ate three pounds each of potatoes per day. Potatoes were nourishing and simple to cook. They ate little other than potatoes. Without potatoes there was nothing for the starving poor to eat. Starvation was rampant and in their weakened condition people had little resistance to diseases like cholera and typhus. More than one million Irish men, women, and children died of starvation during the Famine years.

At the time of the first failure most of the subsistence farmers lived in rural areas on very small farms which were rented from larger farmers and landlords. Many had enough land to grow crops other than potatoes but these were considered as 'cash crops'. Agricultural produce (oats and barley), grown in Ireland was exported to England during the Famine years. The poorest farmers were caught in an impossible situation, they had to sell these crops to pay rent and many were evicted from their homes for not paying the rent. Without a patch of land to grow potatoes, a family starved.

Deaths were highest where the population of poorest subsistence farmers and labourers was most dense. Landless labourers died in their tens of thousands but very few areas escaped entirely and tradesmen, shopkeepers, townspeople and more profitable farmers perished from the effects of the diseases spread by the starving and destitute.

Emigration or entering the workhouse was the only option left to a lot of people. During these years over one million, men women and children, emigrated and the huge new workhouses were crammed with the rural poor. Emigration, brought about by social and economic change, was one of the formative experiences of families, and rural communities, throughout the nineteenth century. Emigrants settled initially in existing Irish urban communities but, coming from a mainly agricultural society, many were completely unprepared for work in the factories of the industrial cities of Glasgow, London, Manchester and Liverpool. Many more emigrated to Canada and the United States of America. Tens of thousands died on the coffin ships that carried them away from Ireland, and their bodies were buried at sea.

Because of the potato famine the structure of Irish rural society was changed. Many of the emigrants who left after the potato crop failure of 1848 were of an artisan class that Ireland could ill afford to lose. Throughout the 1840s, as a consequence of the unsettled state of the country and the breakdown in the social order there were food riots and a rise in serious crime rates.

The political impact of this natural catastrophe was severely worsened by the actions and inactions of the Liberal (Whig) government that had gained power in July 1846. The Whigs believed in the survival of the fittest therefore the government should not interfere in matters of trade. They initially decided to do nothing. However, Ireland's entry into a free trade system dominated by England also contributed to the demise of craft industries and caused large numbers of labourers, artisans and craft workers to seek other employment at home, and especially abroad.

Eventually, by establishing public work projects, the government of the day tried to ease the suffering. Labouring schemes for building roads and roadside walls were started to enable tenants to earn money to help pay rent but manual work without food was exhausting and many died by the roadsides.

It was believed by many in Ireland that the government in London had done as little as it could to help. Early in 1848, a group of Irish nationalists known as 'Young Ireland' decided the time was right for an armed uprising against the British. Wild rumours swept Ireland, mostly exaggerating the strength of the coming rebellion and the increasingly nervous British Government sent more troops to troublesome areas. However, without weapons, food, or adequate planning, the nationalist movement to violently oust the British from Ireland had fizzled out and by autumn had disintegrated entirely.

The Military Connection of Granny Vandal's Maternal Ancestors

I have been unable to find out any details of military service for either William Cashore or his brother James (Granny Vandal's uncles) but I think that they probably could have served in one or other of the following regiments since these recruited in Scotland, were deployed in India or had Irish members.

1. The Royal Scots Fusiliers was at one point going to be renamed the Ayrshire and Border Regiment. In 1851, 358 of 696 members of the Royal Scots Fusiliers were Irish.

2. In 1857, the 93rd (Highland) Regiment of Foot, supplemented with 201 volunteers from the 42nd, 72nd, 79th and 92nd Regiments, embarked for service in India. Between September 1857 and December 1859, the 93rd lost 180 men killed, wounded, in accidents, by disease or missing in action. 58 men were invalided back home to Britain. In 1870, after 12½ years in India, the Regiment sailed for home.

3. In the 1860s the 91st (Argyllshire Highlanders) Regiment of Foot counted 501 Englishmen and 323 Irishmen in their ranks and only 241 Scots. In 1881, the 91st (Argyllshire Highlanders) Regiment of Foot were united with 93rd (Sutherland Highlanders) Regiment of Foot to form the 1st and 2nd Battalions of the Princess Louise's (Sutherland and Argyll Highlanders) later renamed Argyll and Sutherland Highlanders (Princess Louise's).

4. In 1568 the 94th Regiment of Foot was raised in Scotland. The regiment fought throughout the Peninsular War and was finally shipped from southern France to Ireland in 1814. It was disbanded in 1818. Five years later centred on four former officers from the old one, a new 94th Regiment was formed at Glasgow. It was posted to India from 1838 to 1854, 1857 to 1868 and again in 1899 to 1908. These periods included time in Ceylon, Aden, the Yemen and the North West Frontier.

5. the King's Own Scottish Borderers were raised in Edinburgh on 18th March 1689 by David Leslie, 3rd Earl of Leven. The Regiment first saw action at the Battle of Killiecrankie on July 27th of that year. The Regiment was granted the privilege of recruiting by beat of drum within the City of Edinburgh without the prior permission of the Lord Provost. The Regiment served in Ireland (1872-75), in India (1875-81) and Afghanistan (1878-80)

Additional information on the Island of Islay

Initially I wondered how John Anderson (Gran Stevenson's great-grandfather born in 1783), a farmer on Islay, was able to make a living in Langloan, Lanarkshire as a Spirit Merchant. The following information about Islay and whisky helped to explain it.

In the early 1800's, with its mild climate and reasonable land fertility and with the wide-spread availability of the potato and basic health care, Islay's population rapidly increased to about 18,000 people, fairly densely spread across the island in crofting and farming communities.

Traditional crofting, however, could not the support such a huge rise in population nor, more importantly, meet the financial needs of commercially-minded landowners who were intent on establishing more profitable sheep farming that needed more land and fewer people.

Landowners were now demanding increased rents in cash rather than rent in kind or in labour. They started to uproot tenants who were unable to pay on time, forcefully evicting those who would not go willingly. On Islay a programme of clearances into the newly established fishing ports such as Portnahaven, Port Charlotte and Port Ellen as well as enforced emigration to the Scottish Lowlands reduced the total population of the island to about 4,000 people.

Whisky distilling started on farms all over Scotland and, especially on the west coast, islands. Farming had always been tough on the islands because of a lack of good quality farming land and whisky distilling was regarded as just another farm product. Whisky was believed by many to have medicinal qualities that maintained health, prolonged life and cured colic, palsy, smallpox and a host of other ailments. Simple stills came to be found in most rural homesteads and homemade whisky became an essential part of daily living.

After the Act of Union in 1707, the London government levied excise taxes on Scottish-made whisky. The result was a predictable boom in illicit distilling since whisky was accepted by many as necessary for its health restorative powers as well as being the only means of paying the increased cash rent that the landowner was demanding for a farm. Clandestine stills were cleverly organised and hidden in the nooks and crannies of the heather-clad hills. Smugglers organised signalling systems from one hilltop to another whenever Excise officers were seen to arrive in the vicinity.

By the 1820s, more than half the whisky consumed in Scotland was being swallowed with pleasure and without benefit of duty being paid. It was proposed in the House of Lords that the Government should make it profitable to produce whisky legally. In 1823 the Excise Act was passed, which sanctioned the distilling of whisky in return for a licence fee and a set payment per gallon of proof spirit. Farm distilleries were either absorbed into one of the present day distilleries that often stand on sites used by smugglers of old or closed as the demand for whisky grew and customs brought in tighter regulations. Illicit distilling and smuggling died out almost completely by the middle 1800's.

Growing barley was no problem on Islay and with plenty of water and peat for drying the malt and with as many as 13 farm distilleries on the island it was no accident that the island became famous for whisky production. Present day Islay is home to seven working distilleries that produce world-famous whiskies renowned for their peaty qualities and Kilchoman Farm Distillery, the first new distillery to be built on Islay for 124 years. Established in 2005 on the principles of the 19th century Farm Distilleries, Kilchoman whisky is produced from barley grown on the farm, harvested, wetted, germinated, 'peated' and dried. It is then 'mashed' brewed and distilled before being aged and bottled on the farm premises.

ABOUT THE AUTHOR

Rob S. Vandal was born in 1939 in Paisley, Scotland, the middle son of the youngest member of the family of Grandpa and Granny Vandal. He left school at the age of 15 and had a variety of employments including labouring for a small drilling company that was investigating the suitability of the seabed for the construction of the oil terminal at Sullom Voe in the Shetland Isles.

After reading English at Strathclyde University in Glasgow he spent twenty-five years teaching English, including creative writing, to pupils in a local authority Secondary School.

When he retired, to keep himself active, he began to research the history, and to some extent the mystery, of the Vandal family. This book is his interpretation of the data collected during that research.